ORANGES AND LEMONS

For more than a year educational journalist Wendy Wallace spent one day per week in a school, observing and analysing how tough life is for teachers, pupils and parents and assessing how schools really operate in the current educational system. The result is this heartfelt description of the life of one school, showing not only the problems schools encounter but also how creative solutions can fit around an educational system that all too often can be seen as a straitjacket.

Detailing the highs and lows of school life, this behind-the-scenes look is an intimate account of how people in one unique inner city primary school approach issues facing schools and communities everywhere. Focusing on the progress of individual children, and the enormous pressures placed on members of staff, this book illuminates contemporary school life and provides a human and touching account of major and minor successes and failures. By turns both highly entertaining and surprising, the author's incisive journalistic eye focuses on how individuals cope with government initiatives, the needs of pupils and of the community at large.

As the author says, while some children go to school to top up the life they are already leading at home, others go to get a life. Yet although what actually occurs in schools is a matter of incessant public debate few people know much about what real life is really like within them. That is until now.

Wendy Wallace is a freelance education writer who has for the last five years been a senior feature writer for the *Times Educational Supplement*. A contributor to national newspapers and magazines, she is a former editorial adviser to the Teacher Training Agency magazine *Ruler* and in 2002 was 'education journalist of the year'.

ORANGES AND LEMONS

Wendy Wallace

Routledge
Taylor & Francis Group
LONDON AND NEW YORK

TES
THE TIMES EDUCATIONAL SUPPLEMENT

First published 2005
by Routledge
2 Park Square, Milton Park, Abingdon, Oxon OX14 4RN

Simultaneously published in the USA and Canada
by Routledge
270 Madison Ave, New York, NY 10016

Routledge is an imprint of the Taylor & Francis Group

Designed and typeset in Sabon by
Keystroke, Jacaranda Lodge, Wolverhampton
Printed and bound in Great Britain by
TJ International Ltd, Padstow, Cornwall

British Library Cataloguing in Publication Data
A catalogue record for this book is available from the British Library

Library of Congress Cataloging in Publication Data
A catalog record for this book has been requested

ISBN 0–415–35908–2 (hbk)
ISBN 0–415–35909–0 (pbk)

CONTENTS

INTRODUCTION

This book came about after I approached head teacher Seán O'Regan and asked him if I could spend some time in his school as a volunteer with a notebook. I had been writing feature articles for the *Times Educational Supplement* for several years, visiting schools all around England. Many of them, especially the inner city ones where the stakes were highest for both teachers and children, were inspiring places. I wanted the opportunity to explore one such school in detail.

I had seen Seán in the regional finals of the National Teaching Awards in 2000, collecting a prize for leadership. The ceremony took place in the Café Royal in Piccadilly, in an atmosphere of red plush splendour. Seán stood on the platform with his Plato trophy in his hands and spoke with passion about his school in rundown King's Cross, the teachers and children – how brilliant they were, what an exciting place it was to work and how profound were the challenges.

Seán had turned down similar requests from journalists before, and I waited with some uncertainty for his response. But after consultation with colleagues and governors, he agreed to my proposal. I started in Purple nursery in Edith Neville school, in February 2003.

Schools are hardworking and highly structured institutions, where there is great intimacy among team members. It is not easy for outsiders to find a place for themselves in such a tight-knit community, but teacher Amy Crowther and her colleagues and children made me feel at home through their open and friendly attitude. They were confident, frank and generous.

Over the next five terms, I spent a day in school most weeks, moving up through the year groups and accompanying children and teachers on trips and outings. I went on home visits with staff, talked to parents and governors, and gradually got to know many of the people in the school. It was not an easy period in the life of the school, as Edith Neville faced budget cuts, staff sickness and shortages, children with intractable and distressing problems – all under the shadow of waiting for a visit from school inspectors.

Budgets were managed, teachers found and pupils helped. Over the time of the research, I felt increasingly that what they were engaged in at Edith Neville was something bigger, even, than education. Adults at Edith Neville and schools like it are forging some new role for school, for which there are many policies but no blueprints, little reward or recognition, and yet which is fundamental to children's future chances. The numeracy and literacy tests by which schools stand or fall are almost a detail in the greater effort to equip children with confidence, compassion, courage – to give them the sense of a future that is theirs for the making. This, particularly in the inner city, is the real work of schools.

I would like to thank children and adults at Edith Neville, both those who appear in the book and those who do not, for their trust and co-operation.

I would also like to thank Philip Mudd, Sarah Bayliss and Mike Goldwater.

EDITH NEVILLE SCHOOL

Edith Neville school is a community school of Camden local education authority. It provides full-time education for approximately 250 children between the ages of three and eleven years and has served the local area continuously since 1874.

Staff 2002–2003

Head teacher	Seán O'Regan
Deputy head teacher	Helen Griffiths
Senior Administrative Officer	Joan Williamson
Administrative Assistant	Shugom Begum
Purple nursery teacher	Amy Crowther
nursery nurse	Rachel Linton
Green nursery teacher	Melanie Miah
nursery nurse	Laura O'Donoghue
Reception teacher	Lala Thorpe (Newly Qualified Teacher)

Year 1 teacher	Lynne Gardiner
Year 2 teacher	Diane Austin
Year 3 teachers	Helen Griffiths
	Gina Ottaway (Newly Qualified Teacher)
Year 4 teacher	Fiona Gillespie
Year 5 teacher	Collette Bambury
Year 6 teacher	Zoe Hamilton
Reading recovery teacher	Marion Innes
Special Educational Needs teacher and co-ordinator, ethnic minority achievement and Newly Qualified Teacher cover	Nasima Rashid
Learning mentor	Annabelle Ledford-Jobson
Early years bilingual assistants	Shanu Banu
	Amina Khanom
	Rulie Naznin
	Shavi Rahman
	Razna Begum
	Suad Ahmed
Classroom assistants	Jean Sussex
	Yvonne Southey
	Linda Banyard
	Maria Brice
	Nazma Rahman
	Carinne Wittenbol

Special needs assistants	Maria Brice Ranue Bibi Sue Garrett Mandy Treherne
Site services officer	John Punton
Senior meals supervisor	Jean Sussex
Meal supervisors	Yvonne Southey Shavi Rahman Nazma Rahman Maria Brice Razna Begum Kim Pedro Sue Garrett Mandy Treherne
School nurse	Anne Bunko

Volunteers from local businesses assist in the school.

Children's names and details have been changed.

ONE

PURPLE NURSERY

Rachel: Where does Old MacDonald live?
Adam: McDonald's.

Nursery teacher Amy Crowther sits absolutely still, as if trying to catch hold of something that evades her. Deputy head Helen Griffiths, her glasses on and her long hair up on the back of her head, leafs through papers on her lap. Newly qualified teacher Lala Thorpe eats cereal out of a bowl. Morning briefing is at five past nine; by four minutes past, teachers and assistants are ranged on chairs around the edge of the staffroom waiting for the head.

Outside, beyond the high metal railings that encircle the site, parents are already arriving at the gate in the dim morning light. One African mother has a baby tied in a cloth on her back. Young, white parents stub out cigarettes under their feet and jiggle pushchairs to and fro. Bangladeshi women, the ends of their bright silk trousers billowing under English-winter coats, gather in knots while children run around and between them. Children here enjoy coming to school, their parents told education inspectors when they visited five years ago. Every parent who answered the Ofsted questionnaire – whatever other complaints they may have had – either agreed or strongly agreed with the statement that 'my child(ren) like(s) school'.

The staffroom is part office, part kitchen. At one end there are shelves of ring-bound files. At the other, a sink with a window looking out over the playground gives a domestic atmosphere. Above it – in the non-committal, even handwriting of teachers – a notice requests that dirty mugs be put in the dishwasher. Washing-up is more significant than it might sound. Resentment over doing someone else's could be the last straw that pushed someone here into nervous breakdown. Teachers are prone to stress and this group is no exception. Several people in the room have already had long-term health problems.

The room is small for the number of people in it; about twenty teachers and assistants sit close to each other on low chairs while others stand at the back leaning on the wall. Two of the women are visibly pregnant. All are quiet, sufficiently intimate to remain silent in a moment's communion before the children enter the school equation.

At five past nine, head teacher Seán O'Regan arrives and sits down on the chair left empty for him, holding a large book open on his knees. The 'morning book' logs the human traffic in and out of school, records the visits by advisers and students and parents, as well as trips out by children and members of staff. The head teacher is thin, his shoulder frame sharp inside a sharply ironed shirt, face serious and tired. He wears Chelsea boots on his feet, incongruous under dark suit trousers, a sign from his radical past.

'Good morning, everybody.' Later in the day the head will be attending a child protection conference, he tells his staff. A couple are applying to have their daughter removed from the at-risk register. 'She's still covered in bruises', interrupts a teacher, clearly upset. 'She's still dirty. Still hungry.' Her mobile phone goes off inside her bag and she reaches down into it with both hands, flustered.

The agenda covers items small and large; problems with the way children line up in the playground are discussed, along with the expected arrival of a new fridge freezer and the living roof being planted on the playhouse. 'Living roof?' Lala says, looking up from her cereal bowl. 'Sedums', Helen explains, economically. 'They can grow anywhere.' Later, she will relate the printing industry origins of the expression 'mind your Ps and Qs'. Helen has teacher blood running in her veins; both her parents taught. 'I'm still in therapy about it', she remarks.

Minutes before quarter past, Seán closes the book and stands up. 'Right, everybody', he says. 'Let's get the day under way.' The caretaker opens the main gate and – just in advance of the torrent of children – the adults return to their classrooms.

* * *

Edith Neville primary school in the London borough of Camden is, like every school, unique. The last twenty years have seen the growth of a centralised control of English schools unparalleled almost anywhere else in the world, with the introduction of the National Curriculum and an array of other policies and strategies. Still, every institution remains different. No two schools have exactly the same atmosphere, smell, or even set of assumptions about what education is for. Edith Neville – a small school of 250 children from age three to eleven, with an ethnically mixed population and a focus on emotional as well as academic development – is as dissimilar from surrounding schools as one family is from another.

At the same time, Edith Neville is in a club of about one thousand primary schools serving the poorest children in the country. Many, like this one, are in the inner city. Others are in villages where pits or farm livelihoods have disappeared, or in impoverished coastal towns.

Much is expected of those who work in schools like this one. The Labour government came to power in Britain in 1997 with prime minister Tony Blair declaring that his agenda was 'education, education, education'. In other words, it was in schools that a new social justice could be forged. 'Teachers are the change-makers of modern society', he told a teaching union audience shortly after his election. 'There is no greater social injustice than to give a child a poor education.' Professor Tim Brighouse, formerly in charge of education in Birmingham and afterwards an adviser to the government on London schools, defined the challenge for inner city teachers as nothing less than to 'break the link between social deprivation and educational failure'.

Successive education ministers have staked their futures on the aim of getting more eleven-year-olds through English and maths tests, but school is about more than that, particularly for disadvantaged children. Good schools provide children with security, stability and a vision of a better future. Ideally, they also give children the beginnings of the means to achieve it.

Edith Neville school is just a stone's throw away from heroin-riddled King's Cross, a rundown patch of central London dominated by major railway stations and an associated trade in sex and drugs. Two-thirds of the children at the school are entitled to free school meals, meaning that those who care for them rely on state benefits or an income of less than £13,000 a year. Children come from social housing near the school – mainly blocks of flats built between the 1930s and 70s. Few have gardens and in the couple of pocket-handkerchief parks youths gather in gangs, intimidating passers-by. Some children live almost entirely within the bounds of their flats, more barely leave Somers Town, reporting to their teachers that they have never seen the River Thames, three miles to the south, or caught a train from any of the stations on their doorstep.

Four-fifths of the children speak languages other than English at home – mostly Bengali and Somali but also Arabic, and African and European languages; the ethnic and cultural backgrounds of the children are a litmus paper of world events, with the Asian families who arrived in large numbers in the 1970s now well established. More recently, refugees have come from troubled nations such as Somalia, Sudan and Serbia. Families move in and out of the area for reasons unconnected with education; children leave school at short notice mid-year or even mid-week – and arrive with a similar abruptness.

Within a general picture of inner city struggles, there is great variation in how children have fared before coming to Edith Neville school. Some arrive confident and well-loved, ready for new challenges. Others are angry, frightened or sad. 'Family dysfunction', comments Seán, 'is the battleground.' Children's all-round well-being, unmeasured by any of the government's battery of tests, is the vital precursor to learning; promoting it is a large part of the work of the school.

* * *

Purple nursery is cold, registering 14 degrees centigrade on the wall-mounted thermostat. It is newly built, opened just over a year ago, but the under-floor heating routinely breaks down. Teacher Amy

Crowther keeps her jacket on, over a polo neck and jeans. Arriving children stand between their parents and the open space of the nursery like uncertain party guests. Seven are beginning school life in Purple nursery this term; all were born around the millennium and have now just passed their third birthdays.

'Hello, Najreen', Amy calls. Tiny, with an unevenly cut fringe of black hair across her wide forehead, Najreen is wearing a pair of high-heeled plastic sandals several sizes too large for her. This is her second week at nursery and she has cried and clung to her mother for long periods every morning so far, sometimes banging her head on the coat pegs when left. She does not speak but appears terrified of everything and everybody. Today she moves, with Amy's encouragement, from sheltering by her mother's legs to standing by her teacher's – and is immediately awarded a sticker for her independence.

Kelly, four years old and in her third term of nursery, walks in with a proprietorial air, scanning the space with her eyes before moving to the computer and inserting a CD. Two other children pull up chairs on either side of her. Articulate and confident, Kelly is a substantial presence among the twenty-six children of Purple nursery and wears the badge of class representative to the school council round her neck.

While Amy greets children and parents, a nursery nurse is behind her at a table setting out lines of Plasticine with rolling pins, plastic cutters and red aprons. Nursery nurse Rachel begins intently to work on her own lump of Plasticine and, as parents disperse, children drift towards her and start to join in. Soon, she has five girls around her rolling unyielding lumps of red and yellow and green between their palms and chatting.

Behind them, a bright plastic goldfish lies inert on the bottom of a tank while a pale live one swims around over the top of it. The girls succeed in softening and elongating the Plasticine then try out their 'boats' in a knee-high pond standing next to the table. It looks like play – it is play – but there exists a government-decreed purpose for it. 'Investigate floating and sinking' is on the detailed Foundation stage curriculum introduced in 2002, identifying under six headings the areas that children aged three to five should explore.

Purple nursery is purposely informal; staff watch which activities children choose and which they ignore and work accordingly. But the learning here is planned and monitored as closely as it is further up the school. Even Najreen – moving from one pair of legs to another in the doorway – is making progress in one of the early learning objectives: separating from carers.

The children have a range of activities to choose from when they arrive in the morning. One of the bilingual assistants, a Somali-speaker, is helping some cut out triangles of sugar paper, then glue along two sides to make a conical hat which they can decorate with sequins or feathers. There are counting games and puzzles set out in the numbers corner, and paints and brushes ready for children to help themselves.

Not all the children are engaged with adults. In the home corner, out of sight from the main floor area, KayLee is playing. Dressed up in a silver quilted hood, with a blue velvet cloak over her shoulders, she is a wizard, with a pencil for a wand. She is copying a tall blonde boy, who spends long periods jumping in circles, trying to materialise in Diagon Alley, as Harry Potter does. Play looks unfamiliar to KayLee but she is experimenting with it. She jumps stiffly, in smaller movements than her mentor, holding tight to the pencil.

JoJo, another of Purple nursery's new children, arrives almost an hour late. He comes in with his head down, his father holding him by the wrist, and despite encouragement from Amy is unwilling to come in and take off his coat. He is still crying when his father, alternating promises of ice cream with threats of a day spent at home in bed, finally manages to leave him by the coat pegs.

* * *

Purple nursery at Edith Neville school is a direct result of Labour government policies. It was partly built and paid for by the anti-poverty initiative Sure Start – which has concentrated resources and services for young families in the worst areas of deprivation – to supplement the twenty-six places available in the school's original nursery.

This is a state of the art early years facility. The room is large and airy, with a sloping ceiling and a line of clerestory windows along the top of the back wall. It has a parents' room, with an observation window onto the main nursery, special shower and lavatories with disabled access, and a small office and kitchen for the staff. Through the large sliding doors, is an 'outdoor classroom' – a playground dedicated to the nursery and reception classes with solid wooden walkways and climbing frames set in spongy, fall-breaking surfaces.

The resources in the nursery are good quality and abundant. The swirling magic cloaks have black furry cats stitched to their hems, stretching from knee to heel. The pink Barbie typewriter still works, the miniature animals are sorted in plastic crates labelled 'reptiles', 'farm animals' and 'insects and butterflies'. The puzzles do not lack pieces. The nursery is a created world of sufficiency and possibility, a counterbalance to some of the lack children experience outside school.

Nursery is the lobby of the education system, where children's first impressions of school are formed – and parents' past experiences either confirmed or reconfigured. The government has vastly increased the number of three-year-olds in full-time education; now, in England, all three-year-olds are entitled to free nursery places and plans are under way to get inner city two-year-olds into early education.

With disaffection at unmanageable levels in some secondary schools, the potentially preventive effects of nursery experience – the vaccine it may provide against later school failure – have been heavily invested in. The government's belief that nursery education can increase children's chances of success at school later on is borne out by various pieces of American research now being backed up by British findings. Academics at Oxford and London University's Institute of Education – barely a mile away from Edith Neville school – studied more than 3,000 children and compared their school progress with that of children who had not had nursery experience. They concluded that disadvantaged children in particular benefit significantly.

* * *

All the new children starting out on their school lives at Edith Neville have needs. But some are more apparent than others. Outside at playtime, there is barging on the lightweight plastic bikes. As the children ride the cars and bikes along the 'road' through the playground, three-year-old JoJo steps out in front of one after the other, as if he were playing chicken on a motorway. He smiles as he does it and shows no fear. And it is the drivers who seem to get injured, as their high-sided chariots topple over or they take avoiding action and collide with someone else. When one boy falls off his tricycle, JoJo seizes the handlebars and hops on. The original rider screams with rage and frustration; Amy produces a giant egg-timer – the main tool of conflict resolution in the playground – to demonstrate to JoJo that he must wait for his turn for two minutes.

JoJo's behaviour is already ringing alarm bells with staff. 'He comes in with his head down, hiding. He screams and shouts, upsets other children, pushes chairs over. It is really hard to know what to do with him', says Amy. JoJo hates other children looking at him, even when he is receiving praise. He has very little confidence in his own abilities; if anyone remarks on one of his paintings he is likely to tear it up and scream that it is 'crap'. 'He just seems to be a very angry little boy', says Amy. 'He hurts a lot of children and doesn't seek any adult help. He is used to dealing with things aggressively, and on his own.'

The risk is that for some children, starting school earlier just means that school failure begins earlier. The expansion of nursery places has been accompanied by a trickle of newspaper stories about 3-year-olds excluded from nurseries for violent or anti-social behaviour. Out-of-control three-year-olds, although smaller than their older counterparts, are not necessarily any easier to manage. The challenge for the workers is to make all the children successful.

Najreen is also causing anxiety. Out in the chill winter air, she sticks close to the nursery door in her unsuitable shoes, her body rigid. She is, in the terminology of the Department for Education and Skills (DfES), 'new to English'. But Najreen doesn't speak in her first language – Bengali – either, prompting staff to wonder what lies behind her silence. So far, the only thing that has encouraged her to vocalise is the nursery nurse from the other nursery, Laura O'Donoghue, who wears bright and regularly replenished lipstick, who has white even teeth and a loud voice, whose mouth is constantly moving.

Noticing this, Amy has brought in a lipstick for her. Now Najreen's activity of choice is to stand in front of the mirror in the home corner, the lipstick stuck in her fist like a cudgel, applying it over and around her mouth. Such is her fascination with this activity, staff are wondering whether she has ever seen herself in a mirror before. In less than two weeks at nursery, Najreen's confidence has increased. When not applying lipstick, she wanders round behind Amy, one hand outstretched towards the backs of her legs. When Amy sits down to read a story, Najreen stands next to her, leaning her body against her teacher as if she were a doorframe.

But Najreen often arrives late, or not at all. Her mother, young and gentle, tells staff she has been asleep, or has lost track of time. The team think she may be depressed; she is newly arrived in England and coping alone with three small children.

Before lunch, the children gather on the carpet for story time. The circle joins them as equals around its perimeter. In line with the week's 'floating and sinking' topic, Amy reads an incremental tale of animals piling in one after the other on to a small craft. She gets the children to identify what is in the pictures – cow, sheep, goat – as she goes along. Kelly and some others can identify all the animals by their English names; others know none of them. But they don't have to speak English to understand Amy. The children look up at her, make eye contact, smile.

Najreen sits at her feet, applying lipstick blind, moving the silver tube around her mouth. On the far side of the circle KayLee is cross-legged, holding a rag doll with yellow wool hair on her lap, feeling the lengths of twisted wool with the tips of her fingers, her eyes closed. JoJo, for the second time, throws a large plastic car across the space of the circle, narrowly missing another child. He is lifted out bodily by Rachel, his bare stretched midriff emerging between his hooded top and his jeans.

Seconds later he returns at a run, pursued by the nursery nurse. Amy appears not to notice. She continues her high-energy rendering of the book. 'Who sank the boat?' she asks. They're all in the water now, in the story. 'Swim, KayLee! Swim, swim, swim', she's calling, as if both their lives depended on it. 'Who sank the boat? Not the cow, not the donkey, not the goat. It was the MOUSE!' Amy and Najreen get on to the tablecloth spread out in the middle of the circle and to a chorus of 'row, row, row your boat' they all rock backwards and forwards, singing that life is but a dream. By the end, JoJo is sitting on Rachel's lap, watching.

* * *

Amy Crowther, a geography graduate, was destined for a career in town planning until she helped out at a school one day and found she loved it. Clearly gifted, the idea that she might not have been a teacher seems shocking. But will teaching keep her?

At midday, with the children seen into the hall for lunch, the nursery staff gather in their small office. JoJo's name appears on the staffroom wall, as if the staff can't get away from him anywhere. He can't have anything with additives in it; they make him 'hyper'. The staff agree that nursery nurse Rachel – as his key worker – will see JoJo's mum. 'Will you ask her if she reads to him at home?' Amy says. 'He seems interested in stories but . . .' She trails off.

Many of the children have prohibitions of one sort or another. Included on the list on the wall are: oats, perfume, lamb, cow, wheat, nuts, ice-cream. The dust in the air from the huge redevelopment around nearby King's Cross – where a channel tunnel rail link is being constructed – is worsening children's asthma, and adults'. Laura, the vivid-lipped nursery nurse, is uncharacteristically subdued and suffering from chest problems. There's a picture on the board of the staff team around a long restaurant table – Rulie Naznin with her hair out of its ponytail, everyone smiling. But that was at Christmas. Now it is four weeks into the spring term and the hard work of settling in new children is taking its toll.

Amy trained at Liverpool University, doing the one-year Post Graduate Certificate in Education (PGCE) after her degree. Her first job was in Liverpool but after two years she came with her boyfriend to London and got a job at a primary school in suburban north London. After two years there, which included her first taste of management and an Ofsted inspection, she applied for her current job, as Foundation stage co-ordinator at Edith Neville.

Purple nursery was newly built then, and her entrance to the school was difficult. 'It was an empty shell, with no furniture, no toys, no children', she says. There was some resentment that the new teacher and nursery nurse (Amy and Rachel came together from their previous school) had the brand new nursery; on top of which, Amy, only 26 years old, had the task of introducing the new Foundation stage curriculum, with its emphasis on learning through play. She was the youngest member of the team, its manager, and keen to make sweeping changes. 'The nursery was well run but formal', she says. 'They had a much smaller playground than they have now, set milk times, there wasn't as much freedom for teaching independent skills. I changed the planning format, assessments, what happened at lunchtime. I don't think I was very sensitive to what was going well – only what was not. And the fact that I was the youngest attracted some comment.'

Now the team is strong, despite inevitable tensions between individuals. Amy comes back to the planning they're trying to do while the others in the room move into a discussion of if you can tell by watching a child put on his coat whether he is left or right handed. JoJo's temper comes up again, the way when someone tried to ease his jumper off he began shouting at her to 'fucking get it off my fucking head'.

Many of the children need one to one attention, for their behaviour, their speech, their toilet training. At just three, some struggle to cope with a school day more than six hours long. One boy can barely stay awake. Another is worryingly small, despite having two parents of average height. Behaviour tends to deteriorate in the afternoons, as children get tired. Whereas one adult to thirteen children is the legal minimum ratio in a nursery, here they have four adults for twenty-six children. 'I don't know how I'd cope otherwise', says Amy.

The job is undoubtedly demanding. Amy Crowther and her colleagues fundraise for resources and trips for the children; the budget is always insufficient. As a member of the senior management team, she has to cover for staff sickness; recently a senior manager has been off for a long period, putting a strain on other staff. With Nasima, the special educational needs co-ordinator, about to go on maternity leave and an Ofsted inspection due, Amy is apprehensive about the amount of work that lies ahead. Already, she works from seven in the morning till six in the evening and often at weekends too.

As an extra, she is currently organising the school's Red Nose day event – a whole-school charity fundraising assembly to which parents and carers are invited. 'In a small school, you end up taking on more', she says, neutrally. She has recently split up with her partner – 'nothing to do with the job', she says – and is selling the London flat they bought together.

* * *

After lunch, the older children hold their school council meeting in the parents' room in Purple nursery. They need Broadband for the

Internet, says Year 5's representative, decisively. And a class pet. 'We've got a fish in the nursery and what happens in the holidays is that no one wants to take it home', says Amy.

'Everyone in our class wants a swimming pool', complains the Year 4 representative, who has grasped that this puts her in a difficult negotiating position. The children want more games in their classrooms, they say, more trips out of school and better food at lunchtime. Can they go to the seaside twice a month, they ask, instead of once a year. 'Can we go somewhere that's not Broadstairs?' says Amin, the chair. 'Can we go Brighton?'

Najreen has managed to make her way into the room. She's attached to Amy's calves, looking around the children gathered in untidy poses on the floor, putting her fingers to her lips in a warning gesture. 'Shhhhh', she says, in her first communication of the day.

At three thirty, parents materialise by the coat pegs, looking fuller, more convincing versions of themselves than they did in the morning. Kelly's dad comes on his bicycle, in ponytail and a leather jacket, silver ring on one thumb. He greets his daughter's painting with enthusiasm. 'Wow, that's beautiful. We can put that on the wall.' Other parents are more subdued, holding open their children's coats, staying near the door. Najreen's mum, when she comes, regards her daughter's face without comment or expression. Rulie speaks to her privately in Bengali, asks her not to send Najreen to school in high heels the next day.

'Goodbye, Najreen', Amy calls enthusiastically, still pumping out energy, giving the impression that the day has been much too short to fit in all the fun she had planned and there will be plenty more tomorrow.

TWO

LUNCH AT THE GOLDEN TULIP

'Kill all the animals. Kill the mouse. Kill myself.'
JoJo on being asked what he would like to do at the zoo

Somers Town is known as the 'railway lands', with King's Cross and St Pancras stations on the east side of it and Euston to the west. Immediately to the south is the Euston Road, which carries 60,000 vehicles each day. The lime trees on the pavements here are strung with year-round white fairy lights and the phone boxes plastered with pictures of women advertising their trade. It is not an ideal playground for children but at night, when Edith Neville's gates are locked, some of the older boys can be seen swooping in and out of the chequered courtyard of the British Library on their bikes, swerving away on the pavement from under the wheels of buses and juggernauts.

Despite its proximity to the British Library, the railway stations, the City, Somers Town is a dense and parochial urban village, dominated by early forms of social housing – substantial, balconied blocks of flats of four or five stories, built around large courtyards. Only a couple of streets of nineteenth-century terraced houses remain of the original Somers Town (named after Baron Somers of Evesham, on whose marshy land they stood) and they represent almost the only privately owned accommodation of the area. The flats predominantly belong to the St Pancras Housing Association and Camden council and not many tenants here have ever exercised their right to buy.

This patch of South Camden made national headlines in 2002, when local resident Anthony Hardy put out the dismembered bodies of two women in black plastic rubbish sacks. Local papers carry occasional stories of crack houses, muggings and the sporting ups and downs of school teams, but for the most part life in Somers Town goes unremarked by the outside world. With its corner-shop wares of alcohol, lottery cards and sacks of onions, its boarded-up pub and battered public gardens where vandalised shrubs lie with their roots tilting to the sky, it is simultaneously in the heart of the capital and isolated from it.

Edith Neville school, in a low-rise clearing in the middle of Somers Town, has a catchment area of about a mile's radius and recruits children from the flats that surround the school. Places are given on the basis of special needs that can best be met here (this accounts for just one or two children each year), siblings at school and then proximity.

Schools' performances in the league tables are inextricably bound up with their pupil populations. Motivated parents move house to be in the catchment area of successful schools, or attend church services to secure places at good church schools. Unpopular schools often have empty places – which means that they take children who are excluded from other schools, or newly arrived in the country, or the area, with all the associated extra needs that this implies. Too easily, schools can get into a vicious circle in which a poor reputation and surplus places mean that they end up serving a disproportionate number of children with social or behavioural problems. Their place in the all-important league tables then slips further – compounding the lack of confidence concerned parents feel, making it more difficult to attract and keep staff, and attracting the attention of inspectors.

Edith Neville has long been known as 'the poor school', for which it is currently fair to read 'the Muslim school'. The two other primary schools in Somers Town are both church schools. Church schools are generally regarded as better than community schools; many parents who are not religious choose them for their uniforms, traditional values and associated strict discipline. Parents in Somers Town are no exception. Every year, several children start in Edith Neville's nursery then transfer to one of the church schools for Reception class.

In recent years, excellent test results and a positive reputation in the area mean that Edith Neville's star is rising, with twice as many applications for Reception class as places. White and Afro-Caribbean children are both ethnic minorities at the school, where most of the pupils are Muslims from Asia and north and east Africa.

* * *

Seán O'Regan's office window is boarded up, giving the school an injured look. Overnight, one recent weekend, the window was broken, the concertina bars forced and his computer stolen. Window, bars and monitor were replaced and the robbery was immediately repeated. 'They assumed we would have bought a smart new monitor with the insurance money', he says. 'But we hadn't. It was just another shabby old one.' The caretaker suspects two brothers who used to be at the school.

With the window boarded up, the office is dim and bunker-like. Seán's degree certificate – in politics, philosophy and economics, from Oxford University – is framed on the wall, along with a Picasso drawing of children. There are two doors into the office; one – its handle set at child height – leads out towards the classrooms. The other – handle at adult height – connects his office with that of the school secretary, Joan Williamson. Knocks come constantly to both doors. His in-tray is piled high and his desk diary a mosaic of Post-its, lists and phone numbers.

Seán O'Regan is responsible for the school's 50-plus staff, 250 children, £1 million-plus annual budget, its more than 40 management policies, and the effective functioning of the school as an educational institution. He is not alone. Joan Williamson has taken a qualification in financial management to enable her to act as bursar as well as school secretary. Deputy head Helen Griffiths has two non-teaching days each week to share in the leadership role, and four teachers are members of the senior management team, in posts with a range of responsibilities. Edith Neville has a supportive seventeen-member governing body and an excellent chair of governors. The local education authority is in the background, offering various kinds of support and services, some more helpful than others.

But responsibility lies mainly with Seán, in this small office, and this year is a stressful one. Expecting Ofsted puts a strain on all the staff as they wait for the brown envelope that contains notification of the date of the inspection. Funding cuts – a national issue, but affecting London schools worst – mean that Edith Neville stands to lose staff over the next financial year.

Two senior teachers, including Seán's wife Nasima, the special educational needs co-ordinator, are about to go on maternity leave. Providing cover for them will be expensive, make extra work for colleagues – and their absence means that inspectors will not see the school at its best.

On top of all this, a number of children at the school have exceptionally worrying problems at home. 'We have some very difficult parents presently', says Seán. 'There are live and ongoing issues.'

* * *

Seán's day is a relentless tide of events and demands. There are two new faces in the staffroom when he takes the morning briefing. One is Najreen's, sitting next to nursery teacher Amy Crowther, in a red velvet party dress, eating Marmite toast. Her mother got confused about the time and brought her in an hour early. The other is the supply teacher who has come to stand in with Year 4, unaware as yet that this is the most difficult class in the school. There is a new face on the noticeboard as well – a colour snapshot of a middle-aged man on a beach, wearing a straw hat and summer holiday smile. On no account must his granddaughter be surrendered to him, instructs the note underneath. Several children are under active threat of abduction by family members.

Seán, on this spring weekday, has been at school since just after eight o'clock. Year 4 will be an anxiety all day; two boys in the class have extremely challenging behaviour and supply teachers, with no relationships with the children, can find it almost impossible to control a highly-strung class. One riotous day can set back the whole group for a week afterwards. After morning briefing, Seán visits Year

4 to remind them of the Golden Rules – 'Do respect everyone's body and feelings! Don't hurt anyone's body or feelings!' – and to ask them to be helpful.

He moves from there to the school kitchen, where the cook, surrounded by giant tins of meatballs and vegetable ravioli, is in crisis. The kitchen is clean and smells of bleach and recent cigarettes. But there is a problem with staff. One member of the team has just gone on maternity leave. Another fell and broke her arm in two places. Agency staff are useless, says the cook. 'I'm doing everything myself and the heat from this kitchen is unbearable.' Seán promises to see what he can do.

At nine thirty, he has a meeting with a parent. She complains that people in the school are talking about her, after two of her children were picked up by the police in nearby Camden town market and driven home in a Panda car. 'No one on the staff is saying bad things about you', Seán tells her. But the woman is adamant that one of the teaching assistants has been talking about her, saying she is a bad mother. 'I am refugee', says the woman. 'I don't have English. I know very well that if anything happens to my children, no one can help me.' Seán leans forward across the low table, listening, ignoring the knocks that come to the doors on both sides of his office. By the time she stands up to leave half an hour later, the mother is mollified. 'I like this school. My children like this school', she says, as she goes.

Another parent is straight in after her, asking for a job, followed by Helen Griffiths, who wants to discuss a child who has come to school today with an injury to her face, and said that her father hit her. The man is newly alone with two younger children and two teenagers. 'I think he's having a really hard time parenting them', Helen says, perched on the corner of the desk, eating her breakfast of a carton of ready-prepared pineapple. They decide that the class teacher will monitor the child and if there are any more 'marks or lumps' they will make a referral to social services. Meanwhile, Seán suggests Sure Start. 'They do have interpreters. They're only up the road.' Seán is in charge of child protection at the school; all schools have to have someone in this role, which carries onerous responsibilities.

Seán and Helen move to talking about one of the troubled boys in Year 4; a few days ago, his mother sent him to stay with his father, saying she could not cope with him. Now the father, recently out of prison and unstable himself, has thrown him out and said he wants nothing more to do with him. The boy has come to school today but is uncooperative and angry. They look sad when they talk about him. 'He was doing so well . . .', Seán says. A soft knock at the door reveals two small girls holding hands. 'We can't behave, Seán', says one. He squats down in the doorway, asks them to go and wait in Joan's office. Another child knocks on the door, to say there has been an incident in Year 4. Helen departs to sort it out. Seán responds to a polite adult tap on the other door. It is Amy, feeling dizzy and sick. He tells her to go home.

Outside, Joan Williamson is going through the budget with an official from Camden council. Eighty-five per cent of the money goes on staff salaries and this year the amount they have to spend is down in real terms by about £100,000. 'Please pay Joan for your personal phone calls', says a notice on her wall. But the minor economies in place all over the school – staff paying for their own tea, coffee and personal photocopies, buying materials for projects out of their own pockets – are not enough. They have balanced the books this year by not replacing a departing teacher whose job was supporting children with English as a second language, by postponing their plans for a new library, and generally trimming an already tight budget.

Helen's non-contact management time is under threat, and they have an unfeasibly slender £6,000 contingency budget for the year ahead. 'Realistically, the government can't allow this to continue', says the local education authority official. 'Is there any chance of getting any external funding?'

They are already going out and getting external funding, and have been for years. Seán, who speaks with passion about Edith Neville and the children, is good at charming donors, jumping through the necessary hoops for five thousand pounds here to support literacy, a hundred pounds there to buy outdoor games for the nursery playground. But this is time-consuming work and not guaranteed to bring results. It is left to Joan Williamson – once a pupil at this school herself – to state the obvious to the man from the local education authority. 'We shouldn't have to do fundraising', she says briskly. 'We've got enough to do.'

Back in his office, Seán leaves messages on the answerphones of two promising-sounding newly qualified teachers; the difference in cost between an NQT and a long-term supply teacher is around £14,000 per year. Teacher shortage in London means that good candidates are snapped up fast and schools have to actively seek staff rather than wait for them to apply for jobs. While eighty-six people – including solicitors, former teachers, youth workers – applied for the job of learning mentor here, a national newspaper advertisement for a class teacher attracted only one reply.

Joan Williamson's twin sister Jean Sussex, in charge of the lunchtime supervisors, is waiting outside for a meeting with Seán postponed from last month. They run through recent issues – the shortage of people in the kitchen, the fact that a child was choking on something at lunchtime earlier in the week and no one spotted it, that there are insufficient forks, that the water fountains are broken and that the playground floods when it rains. They come back to the key issue, the quality of the food served at lunchtime. 'It's awful', says Jean, flatly. 'That's a hard one to share with Cook', says Seán.

There is good news in the course of the morning. Helen puts her head round the door to say that the Year 4 boy, who had an angry outburst in class, is now calm and recovering in the parents' room. The new school prospectus has arrived from the printers; it looks wonderful. One of the potential student teacher recruits calls back and arranges to come for interview. But by one o'clock, Seán feels he has not yet begun on the real work of the day. 'Operational management gets in the way of strategic management', he says. 'Part of me feels that peas and carrots are not a good use of my time.'

* * *

Teachers, it is often lamented, have lost the respect they were once given by society. But that is not true in Somers Town. Seán is a highly visible figure in this community, clearly respected and certainly much called-upon. He is known amongst both staff and parents as someone who listens. In school, there is a policy of not keeping parents at arm's length. He tells families when they enrol their children that he is available if they have an issue they need to discuss and, within reason, he means it.

When he walks off-site to get a roll at lunchtime, the Kurdish family who run the Golden Tulip café want him to sign their passport forms, the woman in the newsagents seeks his help with her son's secondary school application, former pupils call out sheepish greetings from the other side of the street. People have telephoned him at weekends to ask him to come and sort out quarrels between families; they want him to approach the Home Office on their behalf, or intercede with benefits or housing officials. 'I do find myself writing to the housing department, immigration', he says. 'People sometimes think I can sort out more than I can.'

In a community like this one – with high levels of need of all kinds – it is time-consuming to be available to people. But the goodwill that this kind of attitude generates is an invisible prop to children's education; when parents feel positive towards school, they uphold its values and practices. When they trust the head teacher, they believe their children can succeed.

The sense that the work verges on being impossible – that the strategic role for which head teachers are paid is almost perpetually beyond their reach – is not confined to this school. Sylvia Morris has fifteen years' experience and is a member of the National Association of Head Teachers (NAHT) board. Her school – Cathedral primary school in Southwark, on the other side of the Thames – serves a similarly impoverished and culturally mixed community. 'You run into difficulties if you don't realise at the outset that the job is impossible. The role is problem-solving – and you are never going to solve them all', she says.

Once teachers were simply promoted to headship. Now, they must take a leadership course run by the National College for School Leadership; the Nottingham-based college is a pet project of the prime minister's. The National Professional Qualification for Headship (NPQH) is in recognition of the huge demands of the job; with budgets delegated to individual schools, people trained as teachers are managing what are in effect large companies, as well as leading the academic and pastoral sides of their schools.

Many teachers reach senior management levels and, having seen the demands up close, decide they do not want the leadership role. Vacancies for headships stand at record highs and half of primaries get five or fewer applications when they advertise the top post. Salaries have risen accordingly, with some primary heads getting £80,000 per year.

* * *

Seán O'Regan has a very personal attachment to the work he does. 'I'm not a head teacher', he says. 'I'm a head teacher of Edith Neville school.' He was born in rural Cork, in Ireland, to parents who soon afterwards moved to Jersey. He attended the primary school where his mother was head teacher, then went on to a Catholic boys' school; he got fourteen O levels. His mother and grandmother – another teacher – warned him off teaching as a career. 'They wanted me not to just drift into it. They were aware of the possibilities I had', he says.

But pedagogy, the science of teaching, interested him. After a degree at Oxford, he did a teaching qualification at Reading University, specialising in the early years. A committed Christian at the time, and a socialist, he believed he had a mission to work with the poor. 'It sounds trite now', he says. 'But I didn't think I had any other choice.' After qualifying he became vegetarian and when looking for a job went round schools asking himself – 'if Jesus had to be a teacher, which one would he choose?'

He arrived at Edith Neville school in 1990, as a 26-year-old class teacher, and within seven years had been promoted to head. He took on the headship at another difficult moment in the school's history. Despite the best efforts of the staff, Edith Neville was at the bottom of the borough league table for its test results. The previous head had resigned and the deputy head died suddenly. The school building was subsiding, and government inspectors were due.

At the same time, Seán wanted to bring about change at Edith Neville, to create a climate where 'being positive with children wasn't seen as weak' – and to lever up standards. Edith Neville was still largely based on a Victorian schooling model as the end of the century approached. All of the teachers and most of the support staff were white, making them the ethnic minority in the school. Five support staff had put in 125 years' service to the school between them. Hardworking, traditionally-minded and resistant to change, some did not take well to the child-friendly culture Seán wanted to introduce throughout the school.

He had personal issues to deal with as well. He had met Nasima Rashid while both were doing Masters degrees at the University of London's Institute of Education. When she took a temporary teaching job at Edith Neville, they began seeing each other – in secret, because it raised professional issues and in their case religion and culture were issues too, with Nasima's conservative Muslim parents and potentially with many of the school's families. They met once a week, far from school.

The evidence of his success since then is clear. He has been appointed within the borough to mentor other primary heads, and won a leadership prize in the National Teaching Awards in 2000. The school has four times been recognised since he took over as having achieved significantly better results than similar schools. Results have risen dramatically and the cabinet in the lobby is filled with sporting trophies. Seán is immensely proud of the children at Edith Neville – what they achieve and who they are.

When he and Nasima got married, local Muslim families were more pleased than outraged, although her parents maintained their objection. His idealism is more or less intact. The job is not doable without some kind of faith. Seán trained in early years teaching and when the job gets on top of him he visits the nursery for a few minutes, to remind himself, he says, of why he does it.

* * *

Education is consistently in the headlines; politicians see schools as places where parental votes are won or lost, and quick changes can be effected. The major initiatives in primary schools have been the introduction of compulsory literacy and numeracy hours, skewing the work of schools more towards preparing children for English and maths tests at age 11. Teachers' freedom to do spontaneous activities with their classes, or follow their own interests, is largely a thing of the past and a detailed and highly prescriptive national curriculum defines almost every detail of what children learn in the classroom.

All primary schools have been under pressure in recent years, but none more so than Edith Neville and the hundreds like it that serve the country's least advantaged children. Schools stand or fall by their place in the league tables and, despite the introduction of a 'value-added' measure, local papers invariably rank schools by their test results, not by how much progress the children at that school have made from the time they started to the time they finished. League tables are a continuing bone of contention between the government and education professionals in England. The government's refusal to acknowledge the context in which children learn has deeply damaged morale.

Heads feel, with some justification, that the government does not listen to them. In 2001, the Department for Education asked all 150 local education authorities and a sample 1,000 primary schools whether it was feasible to set a target of 85 per cent of children reaching level 4 in key stage 2 tests in English and maths. Of those who replied, two-thirds said the targets were too high. Ministers set the goals anyway.

There are now 65,000 so-called 'target children' who need to be worked on if the government is to meet its aim of getting 85 per cent of eleven-year-olds up to the expected standard in English and maths. Some of those 65,000 are at Edith Neville; while children at the school exceed the national average in maths and science, English is more difficult for them since almost 80 per cent are learning it as a second language.

Seán attended a government conference with 1,000 other 'consultant leaders' – primary heads recognised as successful and recruited to mentor others. They were fed 'leadership twaddle', he says, from the platform and a senior official from the Cabinet Office gave a cheerleading speech, about further hiking up Sats results.

The head teachers were given handsets to vote with from the floor, as if they were a quiz show audience, but instead they made a noise from their hearts, a rumbling of objection that threatened to become unruly. The continuing relentless pressure to improve exam results and at the same time to be inclusive, community schools, to be accountable to parents, local politicians, Ofsted inspectors and successive education ministers – on shrinking budgets – puts primary school heads in an almost impossible position.

There are numerous children at Edith Neville – and at almost every other primary school in the country – with more immediate worries than their test scores. Children from nursery age upwards display violent, troubled behaviour, or are withdrawn. At Edith Neville, one three-year-old threatened to kill Seán if he told his mother he had been naughty. A child in the juniors attempted suicide. Others face deportation, or go home after school to scenes of violence and despair. Head teachers must determine their own path through the sometimes competing demands of children's pastoral needs and the government imperative to force up test results year by year. 'The argument has been for ages – "crank up Sats results"', says Seán. 'But does that add to the education of children? I won't be a Sats factory.' On the teacher/social worker scale, there is no doubt where he stands. 'Empathy with children is not enough,' he says. 'Empathy won't get them a job.' He is committed to standards, not test results.

The threat of Ofsted is a constant pressure. The rapid snapshot inspectors take is not always reliable, nor will the judges necessarily see the school at its best. Edith Neville is likely to be assessed with two of its strongest teachers absent, and in their place two students straight out of college. A neighbouring school, St Mary and St Pancras, was a beacon school, held up as a model of good practice – until Ofsted came in, and failed it. That year, when the inspectors called, they had a new head teacher and four newly qualified teachers in eight classes. The head of the inspection service, David Bell, argues that putting schools in special measures brings in extra help and focuses attention on how to address the problems. On the ground, the interpretation tends to be rather different. Schools officially dubbed 'failing' have trouble attracting staff or pupils and can spiral into further decline. 'Does putting any school in special measures help it?' Seán wonders out loud.

Meanwhile, he has threshold assessments to do – monitoring teachers' performance to enable them to get pay hikes – a strategic vision to create, modify and maintain, and children are constantly knocking on the door, sent out by teachers who cannot cope with their behaviour.

Walking back into school with his roll, he is assailed by someone else. A charity has offered to plant two trees of any native species in the school grounds, free of charge. Their representative is here in order to check out the site for a suitable spot. Seán spends a few minutes being lectured on pinnate leaves before deciding that there are a couple of spots along the perimeter fence where something might be planted. 'It could be hawthorn, elm, oak', the man advises. 'Obviously, with English oak it's going to be a few hundred years till it achieves its full potential.'

THREE

RED NOSE DAY

Melanie Miah: What shape is pizza?
Sukie: Red.

A hum of excitement fills the hall, rising from the lines of children sitting cross-legged on the floor. Teachers sit at the ends of the rows, on chairs, quelling noise with their eyes. The light filters in sideways from the high windows, illuminating the red hearts, circles and crosses painted on the children's cheeks and foreheads. It is Red Nose day assembly and the whole school is gathered together.

All the families have been invited – by word of mouth and letters home, with translations in Bangladeshi and Somali – but only around fifteen people have come. A group of Muslim men cluster together on chairs near the front, sandalled feet planted firmly on the floor. At the back, a line of mothers, some with babies in their arms, survey the tops of the heads of nearly 250 Edith Neville children.

As organiser of the event, Amy leads Purple nursery's 'S Club 8' group to the front of the hall to begin the assembly. Amy's blonde hair is a mass of red pigtails, their frivolity contradicting the tired expression on her face. Music booms from a cassette player at the back and the children look momentarily bewildered as they gaze out over the mass of faces, but Amy wills them through their routine – standing in front of them to demonstrate the hand-clapping, leg-shaking, hip-rolling sequence they have practised. Older children begin to clap along with the rhythm.

Afterwards, Maharun comes to the front. Her long black hair is twisted into up-standing, red-threaded plaits and her face, characteristically alert, tilts to the ceiling. Eight-year-old Maharun is blind; she was born without eyes. Her learning assistant, who has worked with her since nursery, kneels behind her holding her hips lightly to steady her as Maharun sways from side to side and sings a Craig David song, her voice gathering strength as she goes along. 'You might need somebody too', she finishes. The children applaud wildly and one of the fathers springs off his chair to pat her on the shoulder. 'Craig David is a black singer', Maharun remarks, as she sits down again in her line.

The assembly demonstrates the cultural chasms children must bridge in their lives. Some have dressed up for the day at home; they have sprayed their hair, are wearing red T-shirts and trousers and ribbons. Others are in their everyday clothes, which for conservative Muslim girls are trousers, topped by dresses and cardigans, a modest, practical look at odds with the tweenie sexuality displayed by some of the non-Muslim girls. The girls reflect their cultural influences – whether MTV, pop and advertising or family, religion and tradition – more clearly in their dress than the boys.

Children from the older years are confident in public, used to performing in front of the school since they were small. Year 4 do their own version of Pop Idol, with brio. Individual children come up and tell jokes – 'Why do camels make good teachers? Because they've always got the hump' – and groups of boys display their talent for rap. Girls sing with enthusiasm, mainly in groups. The lyrics – 'Kissing your body from your head to your feet, spending late nights hanging out at the bar' – fill the hall.

A Year 6 girl dressed up in the red, embroidered costume and gold jewellery of a bride wins the first draw of the raffle; her prize is a morning helping the school keeper. Seán drapes his jacket round the narrow shoulders of the boy who wins the chance to be 'Seán for a day', to widespread laughter from adults and children. When a child from Year 4 wins the chance to stick deputy head Helen Griffiths's feet in jelly, the children erupt. Helen displays her gift for performance, peeling off her boots like a pantomime dame and plunging her winter-white feet into a large tray of red jelly. The children scream their delight as the jelly envelops Helen's ankles, drips from her toes. If the sober-faced men at the front of the hall feel surprise at this form of English entertainment, they do not display it. The day concludes with a cake sale in the same hall; staff and children have raised £400 for Comic Relief.

* * *

Parents' attitude to their children's education is more important to their achievement than almost any other factor, including class, studies have shown. It is not parents' own education levels that make the difference so much as the encouragement and interest they show. Non-literate mothers can help their children learn to read, if they are willing to spend the time to sit on the couch and look at the pictures with the child and talk about the story. Recruiting parents to support and extend what goes on in school is paramount at all ages and stages. But many schools – whether or not they serve poor communities like this one – struggle to get parents involved, or sometimes to persuade them even to set foot in school at all.

Government attempts to foster parent–school relationships through the introduction of 'home school contracts' have not been visibly successful. The demands are not great; the contracts typically guarantee that parents will send their children to school on time, dressed, fed and awake, and will read stories with them and later on keep an eye on their homework. But one study commissioned by the Department for Education found that more than one in three parents did not recognise the term 'home school agreement' – despite the fact that all should have been invited to sign one.

Parents who had a bad time at school themselves often find any contact with school anathema, as negative memories are revived. One-third of adults in Somers Town – double the borough average – have no qualifications at all, which tends to suggest school failed them one way or another. Despite the fact that parents almost universally want their children to do as well as they can, no formula for getting all families involved with schools has yet been found, anywhere.

Edith Neville children speak some thirty languages between them. Many parents, especially mothers, speak less English than their children, and need them as translators on parents' evenings or in other dealings with the school. 'It's all right if they've done well', says teacher Collette Bambury. 'Otherwise it can be a bit difficult.' A proportion of the parents at Edith Neville never had any formal education themselves; they can feel particularly disenfranchised when it comes to helping their children.

Some pupils have relatives working in the school, as bilingual assistants, cleaners, learning assistants or preparing school meals. At one point, seven children in nursery alone had relatives working in the school. This is one effective way of fostering relationships with the local community and making the barriers between school and community more porous, although it brings its own complications if people quarrel.

* * *

Schools around the country have tried different means of involving parents. Walker primary school in Newcastle's Byker district put on drop-in classes ranging from literacy to aromatherapy for parents, set up a basic adult library and found room for a community café. With spare buildings on the site and an inspirational head teacher, Walker had both the space and the vision to give the school partly over to local people. Further south, a mainly white Banbury secondary school, concerned to reach out to the minority of Muslim families, put on family picnics where teachers, children and parents and relatives went out for games and barbecues to play and bond. The events helped build trust between teachers and parents who responded to the goodwill evident in the gesture. Other schools have made home–school liaison the responsibility of the parents, which can work well if there are some dynamic and community-minded individuals among them.

Probably the single most effective means that Edith Neville school has found of supporting home–school relations is through employing bilingual teaching assistants – people who speak both English and community languages. When Rulie Naznin, one of two bilingual assistants working in Purple nursery, calls out the names of animals in Bengali as Amy reads the story, she is more than a translator. She provides a human bridge for the Bangladeshi children from the world they inhabit at home in the flats to the one they must learn to operate in at school.

Bilingual assistants perform a similar function with parents, explaining not just language but culture and beliefs. When the early years team make home visits to families with children about to enter nursery, it is Somali-speaking Suad Ahmed who hears one mother's real concern about her child's imminent arrival at school. (Will there be water in the lavatory for her to wash with? Answer – No. She will have to learn to use lavatory paper at school.)

Bilingual assistants tend to be mothers who start out as volunteer helpers then move in to a professional role at school. It is good for the individuals involved as well as the school. Suad started helping out in the classroom when her second child, a daughter, began school. She discovered she enjoyed it – 'I liked helping them. There were all these little Somali kids who didn't know what the teacher was talking about' – and when the class teacher invited her to enrol on a short course for parent-helpers, she agreed.

Suad spent the first twenty years of her life in Somalia. The oldest of eleven children, she had to get up before dawn to light a charcoal stove and make bread and tea for the younger children before getting them off to school. When she left the country, her younger sister took over. Then the next girl did it, until it came to the turn of the youngest. 'She was lucky', says Suad drily. 'The war came.'

Since coming to England, she has learned to speak the language fluently, chosen her own husband (in contravention of the traditions of her culture) and seen her son through primary and into secondary. She understands both the Somali way of life and the English one; she has known two lives. 'And I choose this one', she says. When offered a post as bilingual assistant, she did not hesitate. 'I have been working in Foundation stage for three years, thanks to my daughter. Otherwise I would be a housewife staying at home, cooking. Working makes me stronger and gives me control over my own life.'

Having someone who models what education makes possible in her own life, and who can talk to parents in their own language about their concerns – whether about their own children or about the system generally – is invaluable for the promotion of understanding and goodwill. With such a range of cultural backgrounds, not every child with English as a second language can be supported by an assistant who speaks their language; there are six bilingual assistants at Edith Neville, five working in Bengali and one in Somali – representing the two main languages of families at the school. Even these posts are relatively precarious; the staff are highly valued but because they are surplus to legal minimum requirements, they are inevitably among the first to be considered when school budgets shrink.

* * *

Hibo Nur's flat is approached by a bleak, concrete landing overlooking the new development around King's Cross. Outside, the view is of heavy plant and incessant activity on the large-scale building site. Inside, the living room – painted a deep rose pink and dimly lit through one lace-curtained window – is incense-scented and empty apart from a squashy three-piece suite, a couple of framed inscriptions from the Koran on the walls and a television standing on the lino-covered floor.

Dominating the room, turned towards the light from the window, is a large board on an easel, covered with children's workings of sums. Six-year-old Abdi's are at the top of the board and below that, in a less steady hand, 5-year-old Zaki's. Hibo has three sons at Edith Neville; her toddler daughter is eager to begin nursery. Now 28, Hibo left school in Somalia at the age of 13 before fleeing the country to escape civil war. But education dominates her and her student-husband's hopes for their children.

Hibo feels positive towards the school. 'They talk to parents, ask us what we think, involve us', she says. 'They tell us "come to the seaside! Come to the zoo!" It feels like a community.' Still, she found it hard to leave her first child in the care of Purple nursery. 'I had never left him with strangers. And he did not speak English. I did not know what would happen to him.'

Initially, bilingual assistant Suad Ahmed translated between Hibo's son and his teachers. Three years later, Bashir and his younger brothers rarely speak Somali, although they understand it. Once at school, children with English as a second language tend to want to conform with their friends and speak English all the time. Part of the role of the bilingual assistants in school is to uphold the importance of children's mother tongues. Even Hibo – who has taught herself English using television and the radio – speaks a mix of English and Somali at home with her husband. 'My house is English first', she says. 'We see Somali as a second language.'

Despite her commitment to immersion in the English language and school system, there is a limit to how much Hibo can help her children with their homework. Her six-year-old son can already write more complex and longer sentences in English than she can. Her husband teaches the boys maths, and the Koran, at home. She helps them with 'small things', she says, and is teaching her youngest child the alphabet. But her supportive attitude and belief in education has transferred itself to her children, who are doing well at school.

Hibo is waiting for a transfer to a larger flat; the six members of the family share two small bedrooms. She dreads the prospect of being transferred out of Somers Town, and losing the relationship with the school. 'To start all over again is hard', she says. Her children have made a lot of friends. 'I told them to mix with everybody, Muslim and non-Muslim. I told them – don't judge people and do what is right. That's more important than religion.'

* * *

The parents teachers most need to work with – because their children are having problems at school – tend to be those most likely to resist involvement. Some mothers walk into Purple nursery as if it were an extension of their own home, chatting to staff, greeting other children and parents before making a leisurely departure. But 30-year-old Nicki, JoJo's mother, gives the impression of being in a hurry to get away when she drops off her son. 'I'm not what you'd call chatty', she explains.

Nicki's reluctance to linger on school premises goes deeper than shyness. At primary school, she needed glasses to see the blackboard but didn't like wearing them and had hearing trouble that went unnoticed. Unable to see or hear properly, she did not do well academically and at secondary school was put in the lowest group. 'I wasn't very clever', she says. 'I never got to learn anything. Then my dad died, when I was 14. That messed me up.' By 15, Nicki rarely went to school. Despite her obvious intelligence, she left feeling like a failure and unable confidently to read or write. She had her first child when she was 20 and her own unhappy experiences looked set to be repeated when her son began at school.

'He was always in trouble at school, from the start', she says. 'Hitting kids, spitting, biting. He was quite violent. Then he'd get very angry when he was told off and when he loses his temper, he can't control himself.' For years, she was called in to the school nearly every day after incidents in the classroom or playground or both. 'I used to cry my eyes out. Everybody assessed him, and put it in a big pack.' Her oldest son was finally diagnosed as having learning difficulties, and got individual support.

Nicki is terrified that JoJo, her second child, is going to repeat her first son's school career. Part of the reason she chose Edith Neville is because it has a reputation locally for handling difficult children well. Still, JoJo had a traumatic start to nursery – screaming in the mornings, refusing to be left, then not co-operating with staff once she had gone. She resorted to bribing him with sweets just to get him to school, but they make him 'hyper', she says.

Despite her initial anxieties, she has found the attitude of staff at Edith Neville reassuring. 'They just let me know what's going on and say "would you mind having a word with him at home"', she says. 'I've only had to see Seán once, about his swearing.'

JoJo lacks boundaries at home, the team members think, and they need to work with his parents so that the same rules and expectations apply at home and at school. But this will need delicate handling. Nicki sees herself as his only champion. 'His dad thinks he's wild too', she says. 'He doesn't give him a chance.'

* * *

Edith Neville has attempted to draw families into the life of the school through a parents' group. The group's Monday meetings – a mixture of adult education, coffee morning and careers guidance – are run by parent tutor Syeda Nessa. Syeda has put on activities for parents ranging from computer training to fabric and glass painting and embroidery. Once a group-attending parent herself, she trained to become a tutor four years ago and radiates enthusiasm for what she does.

'My purpose is to give parents the opportunity to explore fun things and activities for themselves, to boost their confidence. The focus is on them, while keeping their children in their hearts', she says. Parents talk to their children about what they do in the group, she says, and that boosts their self-esteem. When she gave out diplomas in recognition of the women's newly acquired crafts skills, some told her it was the only certificate they had ever had 'in this country or in their lives'.

The group is intentionally a place of transition; women attend for a while then move on – whether to get a job as a biochemist, as one French mother did, or to enrol in classes in English as a second language – as Idil Farah is considering doing. Fathers tend not to join, although a 'kitchen science' session put on by outreach workers from the Science Museum managed to attract some men; four dropped in over the course of the morning to learn how to make cornflour slime and Alka-Seltzer rockets.

Most of the parents who come to the group are the ones who can also be seen helping out at the summer fair and chatting to staff in the doorways of classrooms in the mornings. Syeda wants also to work with the parents who are isolated at home, who are depressed and struggling to cope. 'We don't say to the school "give us the names of the ones who lack self-confidence and we'll target them"', she says. 'But deep down, those are the ones we want to reach.'

The organisers have tried hard to make the group both non-threatening and useful to demoralised parents. Camden council contracts a nearby adult education centre to run the groups, which are intended as a bridge for parents into education or training. Syeda puts participants' names on college mailing lists, and can bring in an adviser to help them make plans if they express interest in particular areas of study. It is, she says, about 'baby steps'. 'The parents' group doesn't put a spotlight on them', says Syeda, 'like a literacy class would. Nobody is there to judge them and I don't want to impose too much pressure. If they stop coming I ring them and just ask how they are and let them know I haven't forgotten them.'

Despite being free, and having a crèche for younger children, the parents' group struggles to attract members. A dozen parents are nominally associated with the group but only a few attend regularly. Syeda has worked as a parent tutor in other London primary schools in Camden and Tower Hamlets – but finds the parents at Edith Neville, particularly the Bangladeshi women, the most difficult to involve. 'I thought, being from a Bangladeshi background myself, they might predominate', she says. 'But that has not happened.' She puts it down to cultural barriers to women's involvement in the wider world. 'They say "I can't come, because I have to make tea for my mother-in-law" or something like that. In some families, it is revolutionary to go to adult education.' The school wants to give girls the message that they can aspire to be whatever they choose; this is made more difficult when their mothers are leading highly restricted lives.

* * *

Seán O'Regan tries to set the tone for positive home–school relations when children first enrol at Edith Neville. He interviews every new child with their parents, to welcome them into the school and the system, to show them his face and tell them they can talk to him if they need to. Today, he is enrolling a child to begin nursery. The parents – a man in jeans and trainers and his young wife in long dress and all-enveloping scarf – sit in his office, with a slightly nervous air. Their son squirms on his mother's lap. Seán notes the boy's name, his date and place of birth – Bangladesh, 2001 – on the admissions form, and that he and his mother arrived in the United Kingdom later that same year. He records, using his fountain pen, that the language spoken at home is Bengali, and that Shaheen is the first-born.

He secures agreement from them that staff may administer first aid to Shaheen, can telephone the family doctor at Somers Town medical centre if Shaheen is unwell, and may put pictures of Shaheen and/or his work on the school's website. All this the parents assent to without question. Seán tells them that the kitchen at Edith Neville is fully halal and asks whether Shaheen is allowed to eat lamb and chicken. The father says he prefers crisps at lunchtime and does not like curry.

Shaheen has no problem with allergies, does not wear glasses or a hearing aid, says his father, but does have asthma. He assents to Seán's categorisation of Shaheen, for the form, as 'Asian, British, Bangladeshi'. They have no special information to impart about him, the father says, except that he is under the hospital for asthma. The woman sits silently beside her husband, despite Seán's attempts to engage her in the proceedings.

The head commends the way Shaheen has sat on his mother's lap throughout the interview. 'You've been a really good boy, Shaheen. I think you're ready for school.' He takes the family into Purple nursery, points out the pegs, the lavatories, the home corner, the special gate by which nursery children can enter the school. Shaheen, his attention caught by the puzzles laid out on a low table, is unwilling to leave. He will be starting in September, Seán tells them, in Purple nursery. He writes that down for them on an Edith Neville compliments slip, allows the ink to dry, and passes it to the father who folds it into his breast pocket. For Shaheen, this is the beginning.

FOUR

GREEN JELLY

'How can you give us this dog food?'
Edith Neville children, in a letter to school meals contractors

The good education on offer at Edith Neville is as much hindered as helped by the premises in which it takes place. The school was founded in 1874, shortly after the introduction of compulsory education. The Victorian building was pulled down in the 1960s; twins Jean Sussex and Joan Williamson still remember the rooftop playgrounds where they spent their breaks and the way a large bell chimed over the surrounding streets calling the children to their line-up in the mornings.

A modern, single-storey replacement was built on the same site, but right from the start, there were problems with the new building. The flat roof leaked. There was insufficient office space, even when the bureaucratic burden on schools was comparatively light. When

John Craven of BBC TV's Newsround performed the opening ceremony, the chair of governors at the time formally refused to accept the building, on the grounds that it was too small for the number of children. With class sizes larger then than now, some children had to work in the corridors because they could not all fit into the classrooms. Twenty-five years after it opened, the school began to sink into the London clay on which it was built.

Seán was then newly appointed acting head teacher; his baptism was not of fire but of mud. Governors lobbied the council to pull down the building; it had only ever been meant as a temporary home for the school, and as a result of the subsidence doors and windows no longer fitted, the plumbing did not function. But Camden opted to underpin the existing structure. When children and teachers returned from their temporary accommodation in council offices, in the summer of 1998, the roof leaked worse than ever and the playgrounds, in use as a building site throughout, were wrecked.

Over the next few years, the head fundraised for and oversaw the remodelling of the inside, integrating cloakrooms into the classrooms to provide more teaching space, getting Purple nursery built and extending the reception classroom, with its own dedicated outdoor space. The arrival of Sure Start in Somers Town and the ongoing regeneration of King's Cross and the surrounding area brought in extra funds, briefly. But the new money dried up before a planned library could be built; money saved for the project had to be raided for salaries. The high metal fence around the perimeter only stretches three-quarters of the way round the school; the finance committee could not find enough to pay for the final section.

Many children at Edith Neville come from desperately shabby homes and the head, governors and school keeper have worked hard to improve the school environment as much as they can. Although cramped and in places cracked, the school is clean and bright, well cared for and welcoming. Still, the children have no library, the roof leaks and space for working in small groups or holding meetings is at a premium. The water fountains are inadequate, the lavatories basic and the older children's playgrounds under-equipped. There is inadequate storage space for materials and resources, no room for a dedicated computer suite and the performances at which the school excels are staged without benefit of a permanent stage, or lighting – in the hall which doubles as a canteen.

In richer areas, parent teacher associations might come up with substantial amounts for building projects; the community here struggles to make ends meet and fundraising possibilities locally are strictly limited.

Teachers put up with working conditions that other professionals could barely imagine; the single table in the staffroom is used for both lunching and working on, more than thirty female members of staff share two very basic lavatories, and if they have whole staff meetings it is in a classroom, where they all sit at child-sized desks on child-sized chairs. Printers and computers are erratic and the school is often either too hot or too cold.

There is no spare space to house the services and amenities planned under the government's 'extended schools' programme, no room to expand to accommodate some of the extra children who would like to come to Edith Neville – except by losing play space, a precious commodity in an area where most children live in flats with no gardens, around bleak courtyards decorated with notices forbidding ball games.

There is not even the capacity for parents to bring their children into school in the mornings. Seán put up a notice explaining that although parents were welcome in the school, they should not physically bring older children into the building in the mornings as it was causing too much congestion.

Many schools were in a desperately rundown condition when Tony Blair's Labour government took power. Ugly, unsafe and uncomfortable, they were hardly suitable premises on which to conduct the education revolution the new prime minister promised. Since then, Labour has been proud to declare itself as having made the biggest investment in school buildings since the Victorians. Capital spending has risen, says the Department for Education, from £700 million in 1997 to more than £5 billion in 2005. But little of this has been spent on primary schools.

* * *

Another area where the provision for the children undermines the efforts of the staff is school meals. Nursery nurse Laura O'Donoghue picks at a school dinner in the small staffroom off Purple nursery. Salty chips, soft peas and a grey chicken sausage, smeared with ketchup. Laura remembers the meals they used to serve at the school. 'Home-made cheese and egg flan. Proper roast dinner every Friday, with roast potatoes. I used to really look forward to Fridays.' But that was before school meals nationwide were put out to tender to the lowest bidder. 'You are what you eat', pronounces Laura, pushing away the plate.

This is before any changes that may be prompted by TV chef Jamie Oliver's campaign for improved school meals. In Edith Neville's school hall, as in children's canteens around the country, the air is full of the smell of heated fat. Reception and Year 1 children file past large metal trolleys to collect their food. There are vegetables on offer – peas and carrots, a small bowl of green salad and another of coleslaw – but most reach the end of the line with just chips, sausages and ketchup. They hurry back to the folding tables with attached stools and squeeze in, plates tilting.

Two hundred and fifty children eat lunch every day in Edith Neville's hall, in the space of an hour and a half. But the hall was not designed as a canteen. The wheeling-through of cumbersome trolleys from the kitchen gives lunchtimes an air of emergency improvisation, as if the workers are responding to an unforeseen need. School meals contractors promised to remodel the hall, to move the wall bars and make hatches from the kitchens straight through to a serving counter in the hall. But the plans never materialised and the kitchen staff are stuck with the trolley system they have been using since the school was built.

Maharun lines up with the rest of her class, when the older children's sitting comes. She chooses from the names of what is on offer – fancily titled, the food sounds better than it looks – and sits down at a table near the front with the help of Ranue Bibi, her special needs assistant. 'Three o'clock, you've got your chips', says Ranue. 'Nine o'clock, your sausage.' Maharun, her plate fitted with a plastic ring that turns it into a bowl, eats neatly and deftly. 'Did you watch the match last night?' her neighbour asks her. 'Yes, I did', she says brightly. 'Scotland won.'

Jean Sussex, senior meals supervisor, patrols the centre of the hall using a whistle to intensify her calls to order. 'It's a good dinner today', she says. 'Disgusting as it is. The portion sizes are good. Yesterday, they had five chips each.' She begins to chivvy the stragglers; it is almost one o'clock, time for the third and final sitting. The children fold their limbs out from under the low tables, scrape the uneaten food into a bin and escape out of the doors into the playground.

Camden has a borough-wide contract with Scolarest, the school meals arm of multi-national catering giant the Compass Group –

with an operating profit in 2003 of nearly £800 million. Before privatisation, seven people were employed to cook and serve lunches at Edith Neville. Now, four people assemble them; the job of head cook has been replaced by that of 'unit manager' and working conditions have worsened. Year 6 children make up the labour shortfall; older children set out scores of beakers and serve the salad, bread and ketchup.

The food routinely runs out before everyone has been served. By the time the last of the junior diners reach the front of the queue, the halal sausages are finished, so is the pasta. There is bread on the plate still but it is hard and unappetising. The cutlery has run out too; children are using disposable plastic forks and spoons mixed with metal knives. They accidentally throw away forks with their leavings and the contractors' budget does not allow for their replacement.

Quality is an ongoing issue, with the children as well as managers at Edith Neville. Sometimes – as when they prod the softening packets of 'vanilla brickette' and pronounce the ice-cream 'a disgrace' – the children seem to be echoing their elders. Other times their indignation over the poor quality of the food is clearly their own. Ten-year-old Trinny from Year 5 complains that the halal chicken sausages 'have bones in them'. 'The carrots are too soft. We have peaches nearly every day. School dinners make me feel sick', she says.

Lunchtime ends with the unit manager folding away the tables and sweeping the floor with a giant pair of padded sweepers that she uses to usher pieces of sausage, carrot and broken plastic fork into a dustpan.

* * *

As the overseer of food in the school, Jean has a form she fills out daily to monitor the quality of what is served. Potato croquettes attracted the comment 'ideal for making log cabins'. Rice pudding was 'too thick to get out of the tin'. Vegetarian sausages are dubbed 'cardboard sausages'. 'Shapes' are a recurrent feature of Scolarest dinners, although their contents are obscure. All the meals, says Jean, are 'very dry'. 'When do we see gravy?' she asks, rhetorically. 'Custard?' Jean Sussex and Seán O'Regan regularly meet with the contractors, listing their complaints about the quality, quantity and range of what is offered.

Jean Sussex has a feeling for good food and its place in life. She wishes children could be introduced at school to steamed fish and potatoes, cold chicken and salad, different kinds of vegetables, served in appetising ways. She would like them to sample jelly and ice-cream, fruit crumbles and custard. 'Why not give them garlic bread to try for a change, or granary rolls? Cold meats? Proper quiche?' She reels off a line of English staples that seem unlikely to make their way back to school canteens. 'A lot of children only ever have fast food, or things heated up out of a packet at home', she says. 'Some don't have a dining-room table, they're used to eating standing up. They need real food and they need variety, so they can try new things.'

School meals present a contradiction at the heart of every day in Edith Neville – as they do in schools up and down the country. Teachers and everyone involved in the school try to give the children the consistent message that despite the circumstances of their lives they deserve and should aim for the best life has to offer. But the food they are served at midday tells a different story.

Mothers at another Camden primary staged a raid on the school kitchen, emerging with frozen chicken from Thailand – banned during the bird flu epidemic – and making headlines in the local paper. Some schools have opted out of local authority contracts to produce their own healthy, freshly cooked lunches, often with help from concerned parents. School cook Jeanette Orrey has risen to media prominence after her one-woman campaign to bring organic and appetising meals to children in a Nottinghamshire primary struck a national chord. But parents at Edith Neville tend to take a more passive approach. Most leave quality issues to the school.

Meat is a difficult area at Edith Neville. The kitchen has been halal for several years, a decision made by the local authority and which means that no pork and only other meat slaughtered in accordance with Islamic rules is served here. But while this is reassuring to observant Muslim parents and a non-issue for most of the rest, it is an irritant to a minority. Twenty of the children are not allowed to eat halal meat, says Jean Sussex, because their parents object to it on principle. 'We're English. This is England. It's a principle.' The issue of halal school meals is a barometer of racial tensions beyond the walls of the school. Jean – who works even-handedly for all the children – voices her sense of being marginalised by change. 'We don't even get a nice piece of lamb any more', she says. 'We've been completely left out.'

Increasing numbers of children – including a proportion of those entitled to a free meal – bring packed lunches. Some are more nutritionally sound than others, despite a leaflet issued to parents advising them on how to put together a healthy packed lunch. School council member Kelly opens up her Barbie lunchbox. It contains ham and cherry tomato sandwiches in wholemeal bread, carrot sticks, red grapes, apple juice and a small piece of Madeira cake, carefully wrapped in greaseproof paper. It is the kind of lunchbox that children told researchers from the charity Barnardo's that they could only imagine 'posh, sporty girls' bringing to school. Next to her, five-year-old Ali's lunchbox contains a bag of Monster Munch crisps, a packet of brightly-coloured sweets, a chocolate-flavour dessert and a carton of Ribena – the kind of provisions that would not cause children to be bullied, they told Barnardo's.

Children are not allowed to bring chocolate or sweets in their lunchboxes but the rule is difficult to enforce without parents' co-operation; some lunchboxes look as if the contents were entirely bought in the corner shop on the way to school.

* * *

By 2020 more than half of all children will be obese, suggests a report by the House of Commons health committee. In term time, children get one-third or more of their nutritional intake at school. Schools would seem to provide the best opportunity for both giving children good meals and teaching them to appreciate unprocessed food. But research commissioned by the Soil Association has found that typical primary school dinners contain around 40 per cent more salt, 28 per cent more saturated fat and 20 per cent more sugar than recommended for children.

The government introduced guidelines for school meals in 2001. But the guidelines do not lay down specifications for the nutritional content of meals. They merely require contractors to provide pre-determined numbers of items in different food groups – red meat twice a week, fish once a week, fruit and a vegetable every day. The quality of the food is unregulated.

At the same time, the government has reduced spending on school meals; caterers now typically spend only 35–70p per day on ingredients. The Soil Association, which is campaigning for better school food, suggests that double that would be a more realistic sum.

Camden allocates 44p per child per day, although parents pay £1.45. The results can be seen and smelt on the children's plates. While the 'shapes' on offer at Edith Neville may not be recognisable in terms of their origins, they are a familiar feature at the bottom end of the catering industry. 'When a child is offered a portion of "meat" in order to comply with current Government standards, it is rarely that simple. The meal is most likely to be based around a shaped savoury item or "nugget" – typically a mix of poor quality meat and added fat, starches, flavourings, flavour enhancers, colourings and preservatives including salt', comments the Soil Association.

The majority of children eating lunch at Edith Neville do so for free; two-thirds are entitled to free school meals, one of the key measures of social deprivation in schools, and this is much higher than the national average rate in primary schools of fewer than one-fifth. Children on free school meals have a greater need of good food at school than those from better off households where more can be spent on food at home. But Jean and Seán's serial meetings with the contractors result in little change.

Scolarest – which risks fines from the borough after widespread discontent over the quality of the meals – promises improvements. But their 'Camden Schools Update' sounds as highly processed as their lunches. 'A higher spec menu has been compiled with enhanced product lines for onward discussion and consideration by Camden Council. All Unit Managers have now had Menu and Culinary Skills Training.'

* * *

One way of countering the problem is to feed children another meal at school, although as so often in school life the children the adults most want to reach tend to prove the most elusive. By ten to eight in the morning, Jean Sussex and Yvonne Southey are well under way in the temporary classroom in the playground that at different times serves as music room, parents' room and breakfast club room. Yvonne lays the table with patterned plates and matching paper napkins, while Jean breaks eggs into a plastic jug and whisks them by hand. Yvonne puts out the pepper. 'Although it's only Aidan that likes pepper', she murmurs to herself.

Jean and Yvonne have been organising a breakfast club for eighteen months; they take personal responsibility for it, running a lottery in the staffroom to subsidise the budget for beans and eggs. Junior children can come and do an activity with a teacher – maths club, or drama, or sport – then eat. 'There's quite a few of the children who come to school with no breakfast', says Jean. 'Or they've just had bread, on its own.'

A child arrives to say there will be eleven for breakfast, and runs back to maths club. Jean stirs the scrambled egg. The food comes from a shop called CostCutters, and the local mini-market. They spend £40 to £45 per week on supplies including washing-up liquid, bleaches, tin foil and J cloths as well as the food. Sometimes they put in something themselves, from their own shopping.

They started out with cereals, then asked the children what they'd like to eat for breakfast. Craig asked for 'dippy eggs'. But they couldn't make the timing work, for soft-boiled eggs. They arrived at scrambled egg and beans. The big problem was how to keep the egg warm. They do it in batches, and cover it with tin foil. The whole operation is conducted on two hotplates, with a small sink and half draining board, on a tiny kitchen unit designed for a bedsit. Some of the children had never had scrambled egg, says Jean.

At Easter, they bought them chocolate croissants and hot cross buns. A lot are not used to variety. 'We opened the spaghetti yesterday and you would have thought we'd presented them with a foreign object', she says. 'We've had lemon curd to try, all different jams. Chocolate spread is their favourite.'

They would like to target the children who don't get offered breakfast at home – not necessarily the ones who come here – but the teachers organising the clubs recruit on the basis of children's interests. 'Then it's down to the parents – if they can be bothered to get their children in early', says Yvonne.

The children arrive from their club late, at a run. The atmosphere over breakfast is homely and civilised. They sit close to each other at the long table and chat quietly. Jean and Yvonne know the preferences of many of them and the names of all. They eat scrambled egg, baked beans and toast but they are getting more than food. If the paper napkins run out, says Jean, the children ask where they are. They have a sense of entitlement – that there should be more egg for those who want it, a choice of spreads, fresh toast, a cup of tea. They clear their plates without being asked, say their thank yous and leave, still talking, while Jean and Yvonne embark on the washing up.

FIVE

KIND OF BLUE

'Bigger, stronger. Wiser, kinder.'
Notice on the wall of Purple nursery staffroom

At morning briefing, a bucket on the floor collects rainwater leaking through the ceiling after an overnight downpour. The staffroom is depleted, with enough chairs for everyone and deputy head Helen Griffiths taking Seán's place. Sickness has swept through the school, through staff and children; absences – and how to cover them – are the lead item. Nasima has had a baby girl, a sister for Samir; Seán is having a few days' paternity leave.

As she closes the morning book, Helen tells everyone to look out for a boy in the juniors. His mother has disappeared over the weekend, on a drinking binge. The boy's aunt is caring for him temporarily but says she will hand him over to social services if mum does not return by the end of the week. The boy was in breakfast club this morning, confirms Jean Sussex, and hungry. He did not say anything about what was happening at home.

Year 1 children have a supply teacher, as their own is off sick. The day begins well for temporary teacher Dora, a practical-looking woman in jeans and trainers. She goes through the register saying good morning to each child by name; they answer in Bangladeshi – Channa Dam – or Arabic – Salaam Aleikum – or English. With the class assembled on the carpet at her feet, Dora writes numbers on the board, making frequent, purposeful mistakes – writing 5 backwards, or 3 on its side. The children howl their response and she pleases them further by pretending not to understand what they mean. They love it. In the middle of the giggles, Alawia complains of a stomach ache and is sent to the girls' lavatory.

Over an hour of maths follows, only some of which is fun. The six-year-old children are required to recognise and copy a set of two-digit numbers, then do a page of simple additions and subtractions. Jason doesn't appear to have much grasp of the numbers; he guesses wildly at the answers and soon asserts that he has finished, throwing down his pencil and tipping his chair back on two legs. Two girls at the same table, working imperfectly but steadily through the sums, look at him with awe. The teacher asks him to sit properly and he returns the chair to the ground with a crash, shoving the table into the other children.

As the numeracy hour concludes, there is a disturbance. Alawia vomits with some force; a thin spatter lands on the floor and the shoes of the children closest to her. The children shout their disgust, scrambling away and clamping their hands over their mouths. A classroom assistant takes Alawia away and Dora leads the rest into the playground with paper and pencils. Outside, the children expand in the sunshine, running from place to place to take pencil rubbings from the grass, the tree trunks, the wall of the boys' toilets. Jason sits lethargically on the bench, shoulders slumped. 'What time did you go to bed last night?' asks Dora. 'Ten o'clock? Did you have any breakfast this morning? No?'

Dora has been supply teaching in London for two years. She does not want a permanent job in this country because of the paperwork, she says, which greatly exceeds what is expected of teachers in her native Australia. Even if she stays a term at a school, on long-term supply, she gets overwhelmed by the amount of paperwork English teachers are required to handle.

During a period of intense teacher shortage, London's schools have been kept running by temporary teachers like Dora – capable, energetic and outgoing young people, mainly from Canada, Australia, New Zealand and South Africa. They arrive and are astonished by the degree of central control over teachers' time, the sudden loss of autonomy. Supply teachers are paid around £100 per day by agencies that charge schools considerably more than that and pocket the difference. Some agencies give their staff training in what to expect in English schools, some do not. Wherever in the world they come from, overseas-trained teachers tend to be astonished by the difficult behaviour in English schools. Not all survive the classroom and those that do say they feel deskilled initially, as if they were back in their first year of teaching.

The vomit is not cleaned up during break, because school keeper John Punton is off-duty and off-site. Instead, Year 1 have to squat in another year's classroom. It is a small room, stuffy with stale breath and bodies, and untidy. During literacy hour, Dora becomes frustrated by the slow progress Year 1 makes with the writing exercise she has set them. She warns tiny, pale Jem that 'mummy will be very angry' to find he hasn't finished his work. Jem pushes his hair behind his ears and looks worried. A girl asks her neighbour if the teacher will hit her if she gets the words wrong. Jason, getting up to sharpen his pencil for the fifth time in as many minutes, is sent out of the room. By the time Helen puts her head round the door to check if everything is OK, the cheerful atmosphere of the early morning has evaporated.

* * *

Teaching is always a potentially stressful job but some roles, and some schools, are more stress-inducing than others. Edith Neville has a culture of healthy relationships amongst adults and children; bullying is not a pronounced problem in either the playground or the staffroom, which greatly helps reduce stress. The school is successful and seen to be so – another stress-buster. But the inner city environment and the problems the children bring into school are tough to deal with and can be distressing. Anticipating Ofsted – expected now for over a year – is a constant pressure. And relationships with colleagues inevitably have their own strains.

The qualifying year is generally reckoned to be the most demanding of the average teacher's career. To qualify in the inner city – with the associated behavioural difficulties, range of languages and imperative to think on your feet – is particularly tough, as newly qualified teacher 35-year-old Lala Thorpe well knows. At lunchtime, she is in the staffroom, eating tuna salad out of a Tupperware box after a morning spent teaching music, which she is not trained to do but which, like PE, has to be undertaken by classroom teachers. Lala is in her first post after doing a one-year teaching qualification at a nearby college. The Post Graduate Certificate in Education provides a hasty theoretical base for teaching, and limited amounts of practical experience via placements in schools, but cannot turn out fully formed teachers. Lala will not get qualified teacher status until she has passed the mandatory probationary year – in her case, teaching five-year-olds at Edith Neville.

Teaching Reception is always strenuous, because it is the year in which children must be trained to move away from play-based learning and towards more formal study of reading, writing and numbers.

This year's Reception class has two children with very challenging behaviour. At Edith Neville, because of the level of social, educational and linguistic need in the school, there are higher-than-usual numbers of other adults in the classrooms – whether as bilingual, teaching or special needs assistants. For a new teacher, extra helpers can in some ways make the job harder; managing and being observed by these assistants, who are often vastly experienced, is another pressure.

Despite support from the head – 'his door is always open', she says – and colleagues, Lala is finding her teaching baptism both unnerving and exhausting. 'Teaching is about getting your lines right and being the actor. That gave me the most anxiety from the beginning and still does. I go into palpitations sometimes and get stage fright, even though I might have spent the whole night planning meticulously. Children immediately pick up on your anxieties so you feel incredibly vulnerable, once you understand you can be mocked and humiliated. And having other staff observe you as well as you managing them – when you're not sure what you're doing – is terribly hard. If you're not sure of yourself and certain of your own aims, it becomes very difficult to teach.'

With two senior teachers now away from school on maternity leave, and Ofsted inspectors still expected any time, there is a limit to how much extra support the two newly qualified teachers in the school are likely to get. Amy, Lala's mentor, has tried to help out. Lala has had time out of her own classroom to enable her to observe Amy teaching, and discussions with her about her own practice. She has been sent by the school on various courses for professional development (she grabs the opportunity to be out of school), on top of the ones run by the borough for new teachers. But she is not enjoying herself.

Part of the issue for Lala is nothing to do with what goes on in school. She lives in the neighbouring borough, near enough to cycle to work each day. She has two young children of her own and badly misses being able to drop them off and collect them from their school. When she is with them, in the evenings and at weekends, she is stressed and irritable; she feels they are getting short-changed by what she is putting into other children's lives. She has recently cut down to four days' teaching per week, to try to get a better balance between home and school. This means she can drop and collect her own daughters one day a week, and catch up on some marking and planning while they are at school rather than working all weekend. Still, she is struggling to cope. 'It is like being a learner driver', she says. 'You're always going too fast or too slow, always in the wrong place. There are days when you think "I can do it!" And days when you can't even find the ignition key.'

She finishes her salad and begins peeling a mango in a long, continuous strip. She left her previous career – in arts administration – because she wanted to do something more creative, but has already decided she doesn't want to remain a class teacher for long.

* * *

A school is, in effect, its teachers. Schools run on teacher energy and commitment and although they need effective leaders the concept of the superhead – the individual leader who rescues, animates and single-handedly makes a school a success – is moribund. Head teachers rely on their teams; without high-quality teachers in the classrooms, they cannot give children a positive experience, hour by hour and day by day.

A national shortage of teachers – caused variously by the profession's poor press, low wages and ageing profile – has been addressed by the government via advertising campaigns. 'No one forgets a good teacher', cinema audiences were told by the Teacher Training Agency. 'Or a bad one', they murmured in response. The government has offered what amounts to a bribe for those entering teacher training. Graduates who enrol on the Post Graduate Certificate in Education get £6,000 towards the cost of their one-year college course. Teachers of shortage subjects in secondary schools (languages, maths, science, ICT and – unthinkable in this country until recently – English) get an additional incentive to take up a post once qualified.

But the incentives have proved to be a mixed blessing, with some would-be teachers motivated largely by the money. Recruitment to initial teacher training has soared to about 35,000 people per year, but many of the new teachers quickly drop out, burn out or flake out. Better salaries and other financial incentives cannot keep unmotivated teachers in the job for long. A government initiative to pass some routine tasks – photocopying, putting up displays, collecting money for trips – to support staff has had mixed success and application in different schools, with some school managers struggling to find the cash to implement the changes.

The working week for primary school teachers has risen from just under forty-five hours in 1971 to almost fifty-five hours, according to a survey by researchers at Cambridge University. With more school work being pushed into evenings and weekends, the single greatest factor adversely affecting their working lives was lack of time, teachers told Professors Maurice Galton and John MacBeath. Too many national initiatives and pressure to meet curriculum targets were the second and third most problematic issues, in a study commissioned by the National Union of Teachers.

It is not just heavy workload that saps teacher morale. The inspection regime, statutory testing and performance management soak up the hours and emotional energy of teachers – but to little effect for their pupils. Children – the people who motivate teachers – can seem irrelevant to large parts of the work. 'The things which take up so much of a teacher's time are the very things which are seen as contributing only marginally to the quality of pupils' learning opportunities', comments the National Union of Teachers.

'Teachers also regret that pressure of time no longer allows them to engage in informal conversations with individual children during lessons or to allow pupils, at certain times, to pursue their own ideas and interests as part of topic and project work. . . . Yet, teachers regard exchanges of this kind as highly rewarding and motivating because they greatly enhance the teacher–child relationship and provide what some classroom practitioners describe as "*magic moments*".'

* * *

Stress does not restrict itself to the inexperienced. In Year 3, deputy head Helen Griffiths's class, Suad is translating for a big, watchful boy just arrived from Somalia. Youssef does not speak any English and has never been to school before but he does not faze Helen Griffiths. 'I love getting the new ones', she says. 'It gives the children a chance to practise social skills – showing children around, sorting out problems, sticking up for themselves. And we are very explicit about language. We can integrate them very quickly.' At least one-third of her class have joined Edith Neville since nursery; three are new this year.

She keeps strict discipline, insisting that children put up their hands before speaking, sit up straight, put down their pencils while they are listening. There is a lot of gurgling and sniffing going on in the room; one girl has a persistent, hoarse cough. Helen runs her a glass of water from the sink in the corner and puts it in front of her without saying anything. Maharun is in the class, working on her Perkins brailler. 'Ciara's got a cough', she murmurs to her assistant. 'Every single pair of eyes this way', says Helen, briskly.

It is literacy hour and Helen instructs her class that capitals should not be joined to the letter that follows. Suad does not translate as the class moves on to talking about descenders. She moves the new child's hand across the page, tracing 'April', while Helen draws joined-up letters in the air and the children copy her. Helen warns them against turning the number 5 into a letter S. 'You even find some lazy grown-ups doing it! What a load of rubbish!'

Helen has many personas in school. Giving assemblies or paddling in jelly, she is ebullient and extrovert. In front of the class she is powerful and funny, but quieter. Alone in the classroom when the children go out to play, she takes off her glasses and seems like another person again. The job of deputy head is one of the most stressful of all in schools, with much of the responsibility and little of the power of the leadership role. Deputy heads undertake many aspects of the management of teachers too; conflict with colleagues is recognised as the most stressful aspect of most jobs.

Helen joined Edith Neville from a primary school in Essex. 'It wasn't as nice', she says. 'There were hardly any non-white faces. Parents were very abusive. You could never be with a parent on your own, or in a space where you didn't have room to back away.' Staff here she says are more intellectual, more reflective, more interested in new teaching methods and ideas than her former colleagues. But that brings its own challenges. 'It is stimulating. But the drawback is that they are difficult to manage, because they are stroppy.'

Helen has no difficulty managing children's behaviour; class control is a skill that can be perfected, as she demonstrates. She used to have children climbing on the desks, fighting in class, she says. She got bitten and kicked. 'It was horrendous. I would sit in the car park after work crying. Then drive an hour and a half to Gants Hill. I don't know how I did it.' Now she lives in Hammersmith with her boyfriend. When she falls silent, so do thirty children. She commands considerable respect among teachers as well.

Helen Griffiths has the experience and ability to become a head teacher. But does she have the desire? She doesn't want to be a 'career deputy', she says. But she does not want to be a head teacher either. 'I just don't want that much responsibility', she says. 'And society's becoming so much more litigious.' She likes teaching children, working with other teachers, organising events, what she calls 'the core work' of the school. 'I don't like the add-ons, having to apply for this and that money. I haven't got that kind of mind.'

There are personal as well as professional considerations. Helen, 34, hopes to have children. She knows too well how little time headship leaves for a private life. Research by Scottish academics into English schools found that one-third of female head teachers live alone; the implication is that they have not been able to create or sustain a private life around the demands of the job. Equal opportunities have not fared particularly well in school staffrooms. Although most teachers are women, most heads and senior managers are men.

Seán and Helen – like many successful head-and-deputy pairings – are very different; they both complement and discomfort each other. While Seán's instincts are to press forward and embrace new ideas and initiatives, Helen's are more towards consolidation. 'Seán is a very intelligent person and very caring', she says. 'But our visions are starting to diverge.'

Helen had severe flu and bronchitis at the beginning of the year and has struggled to regain her health. Following the infection, she was off work for more than a month with post-viral exhaustion. That seemed to give the green light to other staff to become ill; the sickness rate rose and the school wobbled with the weight of supply teachers. Invited to see the borough's occupational health specialist – an offer triggered automatically by the length of her absence – she discussed with him the possibility of going part-time but rejected it. 'In reality, it doesn't work', says Helen. 'But I still quite often think "this is a ridiculous job. Why am I doing it?" What I really want to do is travel and have babies.'

* * *

Amy is playing with the children outdoors, running up the walkway, down the slide, while they chase after her. Nearby, Rulie is sitting on a bench in the sunshine while two girls plait her hair. Najreen is out in the playground, in red lipstick and a purple top. Najreen is taller and holds herself differently, as if something about her has grown even more than her three-year-old bones have lengthened. She walks around with the air of a traveller newly arrived in a pleasing city, her step jaunty, her head up. JoJo is inside, having an ice pack applied to his forehead. He banged his head on the sink, Amy's careful handwriting records in the incident book.

Inside, tadpoles have appeared in Purple nursery, in a clear glass tank. Nursery nurse Rachel Linton brought them in a plastic bag on the underground from Finchley, from the pond in the garden of her shared house. KayLee is playing with the doll's house, putting a figure in a bed in an upstairs room, covering it with a satin quilt. Her arm is laid across the open front of the room, her head resting sideways on it so that she faces the interior world. Playing, for KayLee, is progress. Often, she simply sits stiffly on the edge of the life of the nursery, sometimes with her hands over her ears or eyes. At other times she screams for long periods, and tries to bang her head against the coat pegs. She is dressed immaculately as usual, in an embroidered denim skirt, leather boots and with her hair newly plaited. KayLee is the best-dressed child ever to have attended Purple nursery. But close up, she smells of cigarette smoke and urine. She is often hungry when she comes to nursery and always tired.

Amy is going to her first social services conference later, to tell KayLee's social worker, in front of the girl's parents, what her concerns are. They are, that KayLee has language delay, is sad and tearful, and unable to play with other children. Amy is apprehensive about the conference for many reasons, not least the possible reaction of KayLee's mother. 'She has come on loads', she says, with her customary positivity. 'She used not even to use her face to communicate. Now she's up to three words at a time.'

KayLee screams with rage and fear when, later, Rulie tries to take her away from the doll's house for story time. Amy holds her while she has the second limb-thrashing tantrum of the day, then goes off to the meeting with her T-shirt still wet with KayLee's tears. She comes back looking drained. KayLee has been put on the at-risk register. But her parents told the assembled professionals that they are planning to leave the area. 'So we might be losing her', she says. For once, there seems to be no optimism left in her.

Amy is making plans as well. She has lost weight since last term. Her arms are lean, coming out of her red vest, her denim skirt loose on her hips. After the break-up with her boyfriend, she wanted change, and gave in her notice. Then she realised she felt really upset about leaving a school she loves. She's going on a sabbatical instead, to Australia, sailing in the Great Barrier Reef. She plans to get a licence to drive a speedboat and maybe work in a nursery in

Sydney for a while. She will be away for two terms and back next year.

JoJo, Najreen and most of the other children will all still be in the nursery, even if KayLee has gone. 'The great thing about working here', she says, 'is that it chases everything out of your head.'

SIX

BROWN EYES

'Jon Snow is my friend.'
Maharun

It is the new autumn term and much is changed in the staffroom of Edith Neville school. Amy has gone; she has been texting her colleagues first from Thailand then Sydney. Melanie Miah, Green nursery's teacher, has been promoted to acting Foundation stage co-ordinator in her place. Senior teachers Nasima and Zoe are both still on maternity leave, as is Shanu, one of the bilingual assistants. The shift towards less experienced people in school is pronounced; two more newly qualified teachers have joined the staff, meaning that there are now four teachers in either their first or their second year of teaching.

Seán has been in school over much of the holidays, overseeing works to the building, finishing off things from last year and preparing for the new one. His desk is decorated with a framed photograph of his baby daughter, Sufia. This term, his son Samir has started in Purple nursery; like every other child, he was first visited by the nursery teacher and nursery nurse, at home. His father makes regular visits to the nursery, where Samir calls him alternately 'Daddy' and 'Seán'. The brown envelope has yet to materialise, although Seán continues to expect it in every successive notice period; the adrenalised mixture of dread and anticipation provoked by the prospect of Ofsted still flows through the school, albeit with a dash of weariness mixed in.

The previous Year 6 have graduated to secondary school; the ones who went to schools nearby make frequent return visits and look longingly through the railings at their old playgrounds as they walk by in still-smart uniforms with large rucksacks on their shoulders. The new Year 6 look too young for their position at the top of the school, as if they can never match their predecessors in either size or maturity.

* * *

Twenty-five children teem on to a Camden council bus for a swimming trip and fly north out of Somers Town, shouting 'canal' as the bus lurches over the bridge over the Grand Union. At the pool, they crowd into echoing, tiled changing rooms, Edith Neville swimming bags slung over their shoulders. Maharun, in a pink costume with frills around the hips, jumps up and down with excitement. 'Pink to make the boys wink', says her teacher, Mireille Alwan.

The noise level rises further once the children get into the pool; splashing mixes with the bark of the instructor, the cries of children, the slap of hands hitting the water's surface. Mireille is in the water too – in tracksuit trousers and T-shirt over her costume; Maharun swims doggy paddle towards the sound of her voice. 'Watch me!' she calls to special needs assistant Sue Garrett, her plaits floating behind her. She makes her way to and fro across the pool, doing widths to the sound of Mireille's continuous encouragement. She misses out on swimming in the holidays, says Sue. 'But that goes for a lot of these children.'

Maharun joined Edith Neville at the age of three and is both a special and an ordinary member of the school. Known by everybody, celebrated for her musical ability, she is a familiar sight making her way along the corridors with one hand on the arm of her assistant, or out in the playground playing catch, hopping from foot to foot, head tilted. Now in Year 4, she is nine years old and learning to use a white stick to give her independent mobility.

Edith Neville school is small and on one level, which makes it easier for Maharun to navigate than some of Camden's big old Victorian schools might have been. But staff have had to re-educate themselves in order to be able to teach her. In numeracy hour, as the class counts out loud in threes, fours, then fives, her voice is one of the most confident. When Mireille moves on to teaching Venn diagrams – holding up a piece of paper on which there are two overlapping circles – Sue Garrett puts two large plastic rings in front of Maharun, sticking them down onto the table so that she has her own tactile Venn diagram firmly in place in front of her. Maharun begins to read it with her fingertips. 'What's this?' she asks, encountering the hinge joining the two halves of the ring.

Maharun is the first one on her table to successfully sort out the numbers and give them their allotted place in the overlapping circles. While the other children write their numbers floating in the large spaces on the diagram, she sticks her braille ones down close to the plastic rims. She is chosen to distribute the maths exercise books;

every child's book has a braille sticker of their name underneath the line on which it is written. 'I'm so happy', she says to Mireille, when she sits down again. 'Thank you for letting me give out the books.'

After break, she begins her acrostic poem with the rest of the children, working on a clanking machine like an old-fashioned typewriter, her Perkins brailler. She rubs out the first word, flattening the dots back down into the paper. Later, as the class study the ancient Greeks, Mireille talks through the video for her benefit. 'You can see Greece is very mountainous, very green. . . .' Maharun gets to hold two different types of Greek vases, feel their narrow necks, the raised complex pattern on one of them, the rough, unglazed texture of the other. At break times, Maharun casts off from her adult helpers, negotiating the running figures and flying footballs of the playground with a classmate's hand on her arm, emerging somehow unscathed.

Maharun's brown prosthetic eyes are so realistic that when she focuses her attention on someone she appears to be looking right at them. But her blindness is total; born without eyes, she has no real concept of seeing, although she uses the vocabulary of sight unselfconsciously. She is different from the other children in her experience of life, but comfortably integrated with them. 'They love her. And she loves them', is teacher Mireille's estimate of the situation. When asked what she enjoys about school, Maharun does not hesitate. 'Everything', she says.

School is at the centre of her life. She loves maths and spelling tests, and is an assiduous student, carrying home her brailler to do her homework on. But when asked to talk about life at school, her memory is stocked with outings to the theatre, ice rink, zoo and city farms, with different teachers' accents (she has been taught by a Scot and now an Australian) and the music they introduced her to. She remembers the 'mind the gap' announcement at Embankment underground station and the slimy feel of the fish she fed to a penguin at the zoo. She can be overwhelmed by noise – to hear teachers shouting is unpleasant for her, as is the racket in the dinner hall. 'Too many voices hurt my ears', she says.

Maharun weighs small events side by side with large ones. The previous year, she sang at the Camden schools concert in the Albert Hall. She describes the new salwar khameez she had for the occasion, the serum in her hair, the fish burger she ate afterwards at McDonald's – and the fact that she asked compère Jon Snow to get the audience to give her a second round of applause. 'Jon Snow is my friend', she says. 'He's lovely. He's from Channel 4 news.'

* * *

A team of people make it possible for Maharun to attend a mainstream school. Camden's specialist teacher for the blind works with her class teacher and two special needs assistants to plan lessons and organise resources. Staff make braille worksheets for almost every lesson, sharing the single brailler with Maharun. Even standard textbooks are hard to find in braille and if they do exist there is usually a waiting list to borrow them from the RNIB library. Maharun is bright, remarks Sue Garrett – so they have to work harder.

Year 4 teacher Mireille Alwan, a young Lebanese Australian teaching for two years in England, considers every lesson in terms of how it will translate for Maharun. Maths is particularly difficult, because it is highly visual, and so much of the teaching takes place on the board. Art is challenging, unless it is three-dimensional. Literacy is the easiest thing to adapt for a blind child but imaginative writing is hard for Maharun because of her limited life experience outside school. Having Maharun in the class has altered Mireille's teaching style; she cannot do spontaneous things with the class or diverge from the lesson plan. 'I would feel bad because Maharun wouldn't have that inclusion', she says.

Teachers can find that children with special needs have as much to teach them as the other way round. 'For me, having Maharun in the class is the best experience I've ever had', says Mireille. 'Having to be so organised, planning how to include her – it's such an eye-opener for me. Every time I see or do something outside school, I always think of Maharun.'

Maharun's ambitions are to be a cook, a teacher or a politician and the team feel a strong sense of responsibility to help her try to realise her hopes. Special needs assistant Ranue Bibi, who taught herself braille after she started working with Maharun, brailles some of the displays in the school corridors so that Maharun can read other children's poems and stories as she stands outside the dinner hall or Seán's office. Ranue made her a tactile First Oxford dictionary, with raised pictures of apples, balls and cars – shaped in pipe cleaners – when the rest of the class got printed ones, and a three-dimensional map of Benin. She and Sue Garrett involve Maharun in Sports Day, the summer fair, the Christmas shows. They have tied a bell to the basketball net so that she can know if she has scored a goal, taught her to skip, walk on stilts and use her body to keep up a hula hoop, and invited her to their homes, to see Sue's cockatiel and share Ranue's Eid supper. They discourage people from using Maharun for party tricks – standing in front of her saying 'who am I? What's my name?' 'We do our utmost', says Ranue Bibi. 'You can't just do bits and pieces. You have to go all the way.'

* * *

All children have the legal right to be educated in mainstream schools, unless their parents want them to attend special schools. But after a major report on special needs provision, Ofsted said only a minority of mainstream schools cater well for children with severe special needs. Teaching in half of the lessons for pupils with special educational needs was judged to be 'weak' and expectations of progress in reading and writing were too low in six out of ten schools.

Government policy is for more children with special needs to be educated in mainstream schools, backed up by early intervention and better-integrated services. But children with articulate parents ready to fight for their rights are far more likely to get the right specialist help than those with less able or committed parents. Too few resources, too little money – even though it accounts for around 15 per cent of education spending – and what the Audit Commission terms 'unwelcoming attitudes in some schools' mean that special needs often go unmet or even undiagnosed.

Nationally, around one in five children has special educational needs. Some local education authorities educate almost all their children together in mainstream. The London borough of Newham, with only 0.1 per cent of children in special education, tops the list. Others have up to three children per hundred in separate, special schools. The tension between the standards agenda – whereby schools are pitted against each other in local league tables – and the inclusion policy remains unresolved.

The scale of special needs has been simplified in recent years. First, children are identified as needing 'school action' – steps to be taken in-house. The next level is 'school action plus' – in-school help plus support from outside agencies such as educational psychologists, counsellors, or speech and language therapists. The third level of help is to secure a statement of special educational needs; these legal documents – time-consuming to organise and restricted to children with the most severe needs – entitle the child to a certain level of one to one support from an adult.

In practice, this tidy-sounding system can be a minefield. Services are almost universally over-stretched and the shortages most acute in deprived areas. In Camden, children can wait a year and a half to see a speech and language therapist. The role of special educational needs co-ordinator is an uncomfortable one, caught between the demands of parents and teachers to get help for a child – and the shortage of cash in the school budget and expert-time at borough level to make that happen. 'At times, I feel like the gatekeeper', says Nasima Rashid, special educational needs co-ordinator at Edith Neville.

Despite the practical difficulties for schools in fully integrating children with special needs, the philosophy at Edith Neville – that they should serve all the children in the community – is sincerely held. Seventy of the school's 250 children have special educational needs and eight more have statements guaranteeing a certain number of hours of one to one support from a helper.

Principles are vital – integration can only work if those involved want to make it work – but inclusion is not a sentimental business. At Edith Neville, Seán fights hard for children's entitlement to support, because without it the school cannot meet their needs. As the year begins, he is anticipating the admission of another child with complex special needs. The boy has severe learning and language delay is not in control of his bodily functions. He has a statement, but it allows for only ten hours of the time of a dedicated assistant. 'Is he not meant to soil himself in the other seventeen hours?' Seán asks, rhetorically. Staff at Edith Neville are advised during their induction not to shower or change children, because it puts them at risk of being accused of sexual abuse.

Seán, moral compass to the school, is holding out for more hours of dedicated support before accepting the boy. He wants to be able to include him but he has a responsibility to everybody to make it work. 'We're a community school', he says. 'We serve the whole community.'

* * *

Children with behavioural problems are the most difficult for classroom teachers to include effectively in ordinary schools. In Amy's absence, Purple nursery is in the hands of Francisca Fung, one of the two newly qualified teachers Seán managed to recruit last term. Francisca is keen, serious, and has opted to become a teacher after working in the fashion industry. She has been paired in the nursery with experienced nursery nurse Laura O'Donoghue. Laura is a key figure in the school; small, loud and huge-hearted, she is loved by children and adults alike.

Both Francisca and Laura are under pressure from some of the children in the nursery. Many who started at the beginning of the year have made great progress over two terms. In her third term at Edith Neville, Najreen is beginning to speak English; one of her classmates is teaching her the alphabet, writing letters down on a piece of paper and calling them out. Najreen repeats them after her with total concentration, looking at her mentor's mouth. She plays confidently at writing, covering pages of a spiral-bound notebook with what looks like shorthand – writing from right to left, Bengali-style. She recognises the name of several children in Purple nursery from the labels on their milk cartons and makes her own linguistic connections. Green, for instance, is 'peas colour'.

KayLee's face sometimes shows a new animation; she is moving up to Reception next term and getting better at making eye contact. Being on the social services at-risk register means that social workers are monitoring her troubled home life to some degree.

JoJo's behaviour is still causing concern. In the afternoons, he is prone to attack staff and children, hurling lengths of wooden train track at other children, climbing up on the bookcase, or on top of the tables. The new teacher, fresh out of her one-year postgraduate college course, is motivated, mature and conscientious. She is working hard to try and do a good job for the children; the caretaker has to ask her to leave the nursery every night when he locks up at 6.30. But no training course can equip new teachers with the instant ability to manage children with pronounced behavioural problems. Three-year-old JoJo not only worries 30-year-old Francisca – he frightens her.

Only Laura, with fourteen solid years of nursery experience and a fierce conviction about what can be expected of all children, can handle JoJo. There are knock-on effects from this situation. The team agreed that for a period JoJo should be sent home at lunchtimes, for everyone's safety. But when Francisca informed his mother of the decision, Nicki broke down and cried in the staffroom. She said she could not cope with him at home either and that if he could only come for half-days she would not bring him to nursery at all. Fearing more disruption for JoJo, Francisca relented and said she would keep him full-time and see how things went. Other team members are annoyed.

The special needs system is getting into gear for JoJo. Amy, in consultation with special needs co-ordinator Nasima, initiated 'school action' soon after he started, discussing her worries about him with the rest of the early years team and talking to the parents to try to form a consistent approach to moderating his behaviour.

She and Nasima then moved his special needs status to 'school action plus', as the in-house measures were deemed not to have had enough impact. JoJo has been formally observed by nursery staff and referred to Camden's Primary Learning Support service, which aims to intervene early with troubled children and sort out their problems before they get worse.

By the time Camden special needs teacher Shelagh Alletson pays her second visit to Edith Neville to work with JoJo, Purple nursery is vibrant with pre-Christmas activity. Children are wrapping empty cardboard boxes, to make pretend parcels to go under the tree. Shelagh comments on the noise level – the hubbub of voices, Duplo tumbling in plastic boxes, chairs banging against tables, electronic noises from the computer in the corner. JoJo, she remarks, retreats into himself in the face of all the activity. 'His disposition is quiet, and he can't cope with everything being busy and noisy.'

JoJo, with his glasses on, is wrapping up a Red Label tea box. Next to him Pierre, a new boy whose violent and unpredictable behaviour threatens to eclipse JoJo's, is wrapping an empty Nokia phone box. Shelagh holds the sticky tape taut for JoJo to cut, pushes his glasses up the bridge of his nose with her forefinger so he looks through them not over them, and sits beside him watching. Shelagh places herself firmly on the side of the child. 'All behaviour is learned', she says. She even dresses for their delight; today, she is wearing a necklace of red wooden hearts, a pink and purple flowery watch strap, striped tights. JoJo is absorbed in his work for some time before, the parcel completed, he falls to his knees on the floor. 'It's good, JoJo', she says. But he does not think so. The twisted Sellotape distresses him greatly.

Staff have observed that JoJo is easily frustrated, and that to get to what he wants, he pushes other children out of the way. Shelagh thinks he has low self-esteem. 'We want him to learn appropriate behaviour and unlearn the inappropriate', she says to Francisca. 'What seems to work well for him is when there are fewer children around him.' JoJo's targets, as recorded in his school file, are to learn to handle his anger and feelings, and to take turns with other children.

JoJo goes out to play and returns after some minutes, holding the egg-timer. This shows he has been in conflict with another child over a toy, and knows that he will have a turn when the timer shows two minutes. 'That's fantastic', Shelagh tells Francisca, 'that he can come and ask you to help him. Praise the good things he does do.'

Shelagh defines her role as empowering parents and staff to work with children; on infrequent visits, she cannot personally alter JoJo's responses to his life at school but aims to set up positive patterns of interaction between the child and the adults, so that he is not confirmed in his poor opinion of himself. She tells Francisca and Laura that it will help JoJo to learn how to identify his feelings. 'You need to be saying "you look fed up, or angry, or happy". Label it for him very clearly in that moment and when he moves out of it, identify that changed state.' They agree that Shelagh will set up a small group of children, with three or four helpful role models for JoJo, to meet weekly and work on feelings. 'It will be about giving him time – but showing he has to take turns.'

JoJo is a likeable child, despite his aggressive behaviour. When calm, he is thoughtful and communicative; at nursery, he spends much of his time drawing Action Man and Superman, covering sheet after sheet of paper with male hero figures. Staff are aware that JoJo has witnessed considerable amounts of violence in his home. While they try again and again to explain to him the mores of the nursery – turn-taking, negotiation, non-violence – he is learning a different code of conduct at home. This throws a shadow over their efforts and at the same time adds urgency to them.

JoJo is not the only child proving hard to handle in Purple nursery. While Francisca and Shelagh are talking, Pierre comes in from the playground and refuses to go outside again. Francisca tries to persuade him to put on his new coat. 'It's rubbish. I'll kick it', he says. 'My mummy is going to punch you.' Shelagh advises ignoring the poor behaviour, and they turn away from him and resume their discussion about JoJo, in rather stilted terms. Pierre sits under the table, talking to himself, then runs outside again.

Two minutes later, he badly hurts a girl outside, throttling her with both hands out of sight of the adults on duty. It is becoming obvious that Francisca and Laura have another child on their hands with special needs. Shelagh suggests spending more one to one time with him – difficult in the busy environment of Purple nursery where all the children need a lot of adult input. She will bring in monitoring forms for him, so staff can measure the 'frequency and intensity' of his poor behaviour – and then decide whether he too qualifies for referral.

At half past three, Pierre's mother comes to collect him. He puts on his new coat and shows her the empty box he has wrapped for the tree and which he badly wants to take home. 'He thinks there's a mobile phone in there', she shouts. 'Jesus Christ.'

SEVEN

WHITE CHRISTMAS

'Twinkle, twinkle little star. How I wonder what you are.'
Najreen, singing to the class

Seán walks along the corridor towards his office with a plastic bag in his hand. 'Evidence', he says, raising it aloft. They have found cheese past its sell-by date being served from the kitchen in school meals. The campaign to force the private contractors to improve the quality of children's lunches has had no results, but continues.

Purple nursery is denuded. Francisca is away with a flu she cannot shake off; she's on antibiotics and has had to have blood tests. 'Make sure the children don't cough or sneeze in your face, please remind them to cover their mouths', she emails. Many of the children are absent; the silver Christmas tree glitters unremarked in the numbers corner. When five children leave to visit Reception class – where they will be going next term – only half a dozen remain.

Bilingual assistant Suad leads circle time in Purple nursery, with the small group of children gathered on the carpet at her feet. She reads 'Bear Hunt' in English, giving a Somali translation as she goes along, then gets the children singing songs one by one. Najreen, with encouragement, sings Twinkle, Twinkle Little Star; she has moved on from her lipstick phase but is still enchanted by dressing up. She is wearing a pink frilly party dress over her own T-shirt and trousers, and silver slippers. She clearly enjoys her own performance, smiling all the time she sings, eyes bright with pleasure.

JoJo goes up last to stand next to Suad. Looking at the ground, he sings Incy Wincy Spider in his small, soft voice that only the most assiduous listener could hear. He ends, as all the children have done, with an exaggerated, floor-sweeping bow copied from Pop Idol. His special weekly sessions – with a small group of children meant to provide positive role models – have begun but so far staff fear they are making his behaviour worse, not better. He is being made to feel special for being naughty, they murmur.

The children return from Reception, excited and chatting. School council member Kelly has been longing to move up to a bigger class; she is already reading and writing and needs the challenge of some more formal education. Most of the others seem ready to move on too; four-year-old Rai is responsible and as avuncular as it is possible for a four-year-old to be. KayLee's visit to Reception went reasonably well, teacher Lala reports. She made a contribution during the discussion of the story, but was hiding behind a cupboard in the home corner at milk time, ignoring instructions to come out. While the other children are excited and chatty after the visit to their new class, she is withdrawn, playing alone with the small world figures, grimacing and talking to herself. Staff are beginning to wonder if she may be autistic.

* * *

Life expectancy for boys born in Somers Town is 68 years – fourteen years less than for their peers born at the same time in the affluent north of the borough. Children in low-income households are more likely to be born prematurely, be born small, or both. They are more likely to be bottle-fed, have a parent who smokes, become a smoker themselves and have or father a child sooner than they would like to. Children growing up in the most deprived households are 50 per cent less likely to eat fruit and vegetables, sixteen times more likely to die in a house fire and five times more likely to be killed in a road accident.

Schools educating poor children cannot ignore their health needs. Nationally, much of the school health service has been dismantled but in the London borough of Camden every school has a named nurse. Anne Bunko has been school nurse at Edith Neville for sixteen years and sees every child at age five for a health assessment, checking their hearing, vision, growth, development, speech and co-ordination. She is also available to parents to talk over their worries; one of the main topics for discussion is children's growth.

Children generally are getting much fatter. But in Somers Town, the age-old connection between poverty and being underweight lingers on. Up to 60 per cent of the five-year-olds at Edith Neville are below average size. Many are children of Bangladeshi origin – who tend to be smaller and lighter than their English peers – and will prove over time to be growing normally but 10 per cent continue to prompt concern about undernourishment. Inadequate nutrition at this age can mean children never reach their potential height; it makes them susceptible to infections and affects concentration and attention span.

The connection between health and education has long been recognised, as demonstrated by the creation of school nurses at the turn of the last century. But the links between fitness and learning are coming to seem ever more pronounced, as new research uncovers the effect of diet on brain function and behaviour. Anne tries to advise parents about what she calls 'feeding and eating practices' – trying to persuade them of the benefits of moving away from snacks and sweets and towards proper meals, eaten sitting down. Children of four and five still having bottles of milk in the mornings and evenings, in place of a meal, is a major issue, as is children who are already small and light eating junk food. 'If parents are buying Coke and crisps, they can end up not eating much else', says Anne. 'But some parents see it as punitive not to give sweets and fizzy drinks and if the children are small they can be glad for them to eat anything.'

Dental health in Somers Town is amongst the worst in the country, particularly for children. A visiting dentist comes to the school to check children's teeth and ask children if they have a toothbrush at home and whether they have ever been to the dentist. 'Usually, the answer is no', says Anne Bunko. 'In Bangladeshi and African cultures, preventative health care is a new idea. They will only take the child for attention when a problem presents itself.' It is not unusual for children to have had several teeth out by age six or seven, after years of sugary drinks, bottles and dummies.

Children's emotional and mental health needs are paramount. Drug and alcohol abuse on the part of parents has a devastating effect on some children, says Anne. 'It is compounded in Camden by children coming from civil war zones, having younger parents, parents on their own, parents who are desensitised or who do not have the skills and support that they need.' Even simple things like sleeping patterns can have a substantial impact on how children learn and behave at school; some under-eights are up until eleven or twelve at night says Anne Bunko, or have haphazard routines. Many issues are culturally sensitive; the health service encounters some African families using what Anne Bunko calls 'levels of discipline that are unreasonable, to our eyes'. School nurses in the borough are each referring an average of one child per week for expert help for mental health issues. Boys in particular are floundering, says Anne, in terms of their emotional development and self-esteem.

The relentless government-driven pressure to achieve at school is one of the stresses on young children. When the charity the Place2Be asked children 'how it feels to be 10', 40 per cent said Sats were a major anxiety, alongside their weight and 'responsibility'.

It is hard to change parents' behaviour – unless that parent wants to change. Parent education classes are difficult to manage effectively and seen by some as stigmatising. 'The uptake is generally quite poor and it has always been the same four or five parents who have come', says Anne Bunko. Often, the parent who is sufficiently concerned and conscientious to come along to a group is the parent who is doing a reasonable job anyway. Sure Start, the government initiative to help poor parents and young children, has struggled to work with the most needy families.

Children 'in need' are seen termly. In need means that there are parenting problems, or domestic violence occurring at home, any 'issues that make you concerned about the general health and safety and development of that child, that cause you anxiety one way or another', says Anne. Only a handful of children are on the child protection register at Edith Neville; about twenty families have 'children in need'. 'These are the parents you want to make links with but who fail to attend appointments.' In this, she says, there has been no real change over sixteen years.

Anne Bunko is far from complacent about the potential of her service to influence behaviour. 'At a very basic level, second and third generation Bangladeshi families are behaving differently. But we are starting again with other groups – from Somalia, Eritrea, Congo. . . .'

The government has said that primary schools are expected to contribute to reversing the rise in childhood obesity – providing a minimum of two hours per week of school sport. But Anne says an hour a day, for all children in all schools, would do more. 'We're trying to build up strength and stop the changes in the vessels. And it would help everything – self-esteem, especially with boys, concentration levels, behaviour in class. Some of the frustrations would be eased.'

Domestic violence is not quite so hidden as it once was; more women are seeking help and if children disclose at school that something is happening – one child was delaying going home after school, staff discovered it was to avoid the violence occurring at home – then action is taken. Still, she says, there is a lot of pressure within many communities for the woman to stay with the abuser. 'It is amazing what kids are living through and dealing with and yet they still manage to get in to school and learn', she says. 'That is what keeps me in my job really. Children's resilience.'

* * *

The environment around the school is not a healthy one. Somers Town, low-lying and surrounded by major roads and railway stations, is a natural pollution trap. Development of the Channel Tunnel Rail Link around King's Cross is blamed for constant gritty dust in the air; at least one in eight children at the school has asthma.

Local residents do not greatly contribute to urban pollution; three-quarters of households in Somers Town do not own a car, compared to around one-quarter nationally. The mêlée of four-wheel drives that afflicts the front of other primary schools in the mornings is not an issue at Edith Neville, where almost every child walks to school.

Housing quality is mixed locally. Some flats are damp, mouldy and in poor repair. Many are ill-ventilated; people near the ground do not feel safe to leave windows open. People in Somers Town live in close proximity to one another, which brings its own stresses. Children from one family at Edith Neville have grown up living above someone who complains every time they make any noise. Each successive child, on arrival at nursery, had to learn to play without fear with 'noisy' toys such as wooden bricks or anything that could topple on to the floor. Another family, in a tall tower block, was racially harassed by a neighbour. The Muslim single mother had excrement, condoms and pornography pushed through the bars of the security gate outside her door inside the block of flats. For three years, the children barely left the house except to go to school. The harassment ended shortly before the perpetrator, a drug addict and prostitute, was murdered by a client.

* * *

While some children go to school to top up the life they are already leading at home, some go to get a life. Nursery children at Edith Neville, say their parents, often spend Saturday and Sunday mornings crying because they want to go to school. Suad Ahmed used to tell her daughter Samira that there was a guard dog in the school, and that was why she could not go at weekends. It did not console her; she used to cry for an hour on Saturdays. Samira wants to be a teacher. She practises at home, lining up her toys, bossing them about, encouraging them, telling them off. 'Where did you get that from?' her mother asked her. 'From Lynne', she said, naming her teacher.

The poor attendance rate in nursery – children miss an average of a day and a half per fortnight each – is more to do with parents' competing agendas than children's reluctance. For a lot of the children, school is the grand event in their lives and the source of most of their stimulation, fun and pleasure. Older children tell their teachers they hate the holidays and can't wait to come back at the beginning of term. Attendance figures, like those for test results, cannot be taken at face value. The percentages are skewed by the fact that if a major Muslim holiday falls in term time, almost no Muslim children will come to school. Families taking children away on extended term-time holidays in their countries of origin also affect the figures.

Many of the flats near the school are small and overcrowded; children watch television in living rooms where spare beds are upended against the walls and duvets and pillows piled in the corners and passages. Some share beds with their younger brothers or sisters, or arrive late for school because they had to queue to use the bathroom.

While television is ubiquitous, books – apart from the Koran – are not much in evidence in many of the children's homes. Toys are often few and far between. The world depicted on television – of celebrity chefs, home makeovers, middle English and American suburban affluence – is unrecognisable in many of the households of Somers Town. Some children's only reading material is the Argos catalogue. Children whose parents came as adults from Africa and Asia live in micro replicas of households in Sylhet and Lagos, with formal photographs of relatives dressed in their best hung high on the walls alongside elaborately rendered verses from the Koran and a few pieces of glassware or china in a cabinet. Kitchens are places of work rather than temples of aspiration and in all seasons lines of washing hang on the balconies. Some children play out on the streets in all weathers and at all hours. Others barely leave their flats; they are what Tim Gill of the Children's Play Council has termed 'battery-reared'.

Children in Somers Town are not spoiled, on the whole. They are resourceful, often kind, sometimes mature beyond their years. But they tend to lack experience. When Amy Crowther first began home visits to children being admitted to nursery, she went to flats with no furniture, no wallpaper, and sat with mothers on plastic garden chairs in flats perched high in the sky. Even children who are materially better off may have home lives revolving entirely around the family, with little exposure to the wider world. Some children sat silently on the floor during her visits, or hid behind their parents. Others seized the camera she took to photograph them with, and ripped the pages of the books.

On one morning of home visits every single family had ongoing health issues or crises in the family – a bereavement in one household where Granny had died and the mother had flown home to Nigeria for the funeral; a seriously ill young relative in another house, where the mother had been up to the small hours caring for a toddler whose own mother lay in intensive care; a new baby and tensions in the step-family in a third household; and a new baby and older child with severe special needs in another.

Mothers who do not speak English and who have several small children and a limited income and live in walk-up flats – whose stairways they may share with addicts and prostitutes – tend not to take them out much; some struggle even to get the children to school. Cut off by railway lands to the east and west, and a major road to the south, children's horizons may not extend much beyond Somers Town or even their own flats. In a further irony, their horizons are marked by the giant cranes involved in the construction of a rail link to Europe on their doorstep. Whether they will one day be among the passengers remains to be seen.

Meanwhile, the staff at Edith Neville make great efforts to give children experiences beyond the school gates. On the annual visit to Broadstairs on the Kent coast, there are always a handful of children and adults who have not seen the sea before. On outings in London, some are unfamiliar with escalators, ticket barriers. London Zoo, within easy walking distance of Somers Town, is a foreign land for most families when they first go with the school. When Collette Bambury studied rivers with her class, some children said they had never seen one – including the Thames.

Trips out of school and clubs provide many of the children with experiences they would never otherwise get. KayLee, on her first visit to Broadstairs, was transformed by the experience of playing on the sand, paddling in the sea, eating strawberry ice-cream. She talked, smiled, made eye contact. On the coach on the way home, she had a massive tantrum, then slept for two hours. The day is one of teacher Amy Crowther's most cherished memories; she keeps a picture of KayLee at Broadstairs pasted into the front of her diary.

This time-consuming and central work – countering the many gaps in a child's life that constitute social exclusion – is not recognised by government league tables, or valued for its own sake by the system. The disincentives – the financial costs and time and energy spent on planning, plus the real risk of being sued if a child has any kind of accident – are considerable. But the outings and residential trips that schools like Edith Neville continue to offer children alongside their classroom learning might truly be described as 'educare' – the phrase put forward by former education secretary Charles Clarke when he suggested schools should look after children from eight a.m. till six p.m.

* * *

Although few put down their names, or contributed towards the cost of the coach as requested, there is a good show of parents for the Foundation stage outing to see Father Christmas. KayLee's mother comes – plans for leaving London have not so far materialised – and JoJo's. Najreen's mother sits on the front seat of the coach holding her daughter's hand. Laura agrees to take charge of Pierre, after his mother decides at the last minute not to come. 'I'll be strong, mummy, don't worry', she beams at her, waving goodbye through pink lipstick and a fur-trimmed hood.

By Baker Street, Najreen is pointing out of the window and counting Christmas trees, electrified by what she is seeing. Ali's head is rolling back against the seat. From the back of the coach comes Laura's voice, talking to parents. 'She's doing water skiing. Swimming with dolphins. She's coming back in April.' As the coach negotiates Hyde Park Corner and pulls into Knightsbridge, the Christmas decorations grow more opulent; the shop fronts are alive with coloured lights and bejewelled parcels. The noise level on the coach rises and Ali wakes up. The doorman at Harvey Nichols raises his top hat to him through the glass. 'Is that a policeman?' he asks.

In Harrods, there is disappointment. The queue to get into Santa's grotto is three hours long and snakes the length and breadth of the fifth floor toy department. Melanie Miah is devastated; newly in charge since Amy's departure, this is the first big trip she has planned on her own. She has thought about every detail, giving out a photocopied itinerary and floor plan showing where the loos are (luxury washrooms, in Harrods-speak), where the meeting point is and asking parents to remember that the outing is for the children, not a shopping trip. But despite her reconnaissance visit and several phone calls to the store, no one warned her that school parties need to come at 9.30, before opening time, to get a chance to visit the grotto. While the Edith Neville party gets into the queue anyway, mothers in thin, unfashionable coats being brushed past by customers in furs and leather trousers, she goes to remonstrate with the manager. Harrods employees ply the queue with Harrods teddy biscuits, and whistling lollies; the children take them cautiously.

The manager does not oblige. He advises Melanie: 'Never mind. You'll know next year.' The children show no disappointment and content themselves with looking at the toys. JoJo and Pierre stand reverentially in front of a mountain of boxed Action Men. They are particularly taken with Action Man in his sleeping bag. Maharun, who has come along for the experience, sits in a real miniature sports car, feeling the leather steering wheel and wooden dashboard with her fingertips, face tilted to the ceiling.

Laura's spirits are undimmed. 'Santa had too many people to see', she announces to the children, at top volume. 'We're going to have our own Christmas party in the nursery.' Pierre punches at her arm and tries to bite her when she takes his hand on the escalator. Outside, waiting for the coaches, several mothers light up cigarettes with an air of relief. 'Dramas', announces Laura, leading the line of children back through the front gate of Edith Neville, late for lunch. 'We've had big dramas.'

EIGHT

GREY SKIES

'Don't Frow Rubbish.'
Year 4's work on the environment

Edith Neville school stands in a clearing in the middle of Somers Town. The low-rise building is well maintained and the grounds are spacious, with a characterful mock acacia tree shading the main entrance to the school. The railings around the outside are freshly painted and the corners and bushes clear of litter. Seán, in common with most head teachers, is incapable of walking past a dropped crisp packet or sweet wrapper without stooping to pick it up. The school has the air of an oasis, a green and pleasant place in contrast to the grime and disorder in parts of the estate.

Parents choose schools on many bases – proximity, exam results, family loyalties. But teachers and heads agree that you can tell a lot about a school simply by walking into it. Inside Edith Neville, the reception area is bright and clear, the walls decorated with press cuttings celebrating the school's achievements and notices of welcome in different languages. There is a display cabinet full of children's sporting trophies, a place for parents to sit while they wait to see Seán or a teacher, displays of the children's essays and artwork along the walls. Although the doors have to be kept locked for security, administrator Shugom is usually at her desk in the office by the front door, to admit and greet visitors.

The school environment is a crucial part of children's educational experience, and the struggle to keep inner city schools safe, clean and welcoming, amid surroundings that are none of these things, falls mainly to the school keeper. Now in his forties, school keeper John Punton has worked at Edith Neville for sixteen years. He came on a one-week temporary placement when the former school keeper was off sick, applied for the permanent job when it came up and has never left. John moved into the three-bedroom, caretaker's house next door to the school eighteen months after getting the job, when the squatters had been evicted from it, leaving behind the bedroom he shared with his brother in his parents' council flat. It was, he says, 'nice to have room for my guitars'.

Although the role is poorly paid and little recognised, there are parallels with the role of the head teacher. Like Seán, John Punton works alone and has wide-ranging responsibilities that never really end and must be carried out with one eye on the budget. No sooner has he fixed one problem than another turns up; a water fountain hanging off the wall with a burst mains pipe behind it, lights crackling in the hall, noisy door stoppers in need of lubrication. 'Stress sets in when I find out what I've got to do around school', he says. 'Especially when you're trying to save money. You don't want the school to be paying a fortune.'

John Punton, like the head, is a point of contact for children and parents – in John's case because he opens the gates in the morning.

He sees which four-year-old arrives alone, mentions it to the teachers. Staff at Edith Neville are strict about not letting young children leave school alone or with young brothers and sisters – there is less they can do about children arriving unaccompanied.

Like many people who work in Edith Neville school in roles other than teaching, John Punton did not enjoy his own education. A gentle boy who loved music, he did not thrive in the Camden comprehensive he attended in the 1970s. 'There was bullying, violence. Teachers getting beaten up. I just learned to duck', he says. His mother cleaned at the school in the evenings; she used to come home and tell him which teachers had been crying in the staffroom after the children went home. One member of staff killed himself. John cannot remember what qualifications he left with but he took a GCSE in English after leaving, to help with his role as school keeper, which like most things in schools involves a surprisingly large amount of paperwork – keeping a maintenance book and fire log, filling in worksheets for contractors.

Now, he is dedicated to taking care of the school and improving the environment for the children. John Punton's day begins at seven, when he searches the grounds for needles or glass bottles that may have come over the railings in the night. But the work continues throughout the day. The toilets, he says, 'get misused'. 'Boys pee on the floor. Or other things. Throw tissues on the walls, or the ceilings.' Vomit is ongoing. 'You can have a week of it. It depends what bugs are going around.'

While he is talking, John is called to an emergency. A child has dropped a five-litre bucket of acrylic primer on Year 4's classroom floor; it split and spilled paint all over the blue carpet. By the time he arrives, paint is spreading viscously around the legs of tables and chairs. He scoops up the top layer with a bucket and dustpan then tackles the next layer with a cloth. His concern is to make the classroom safe – the carpet is beyond saving. But he has to leave the mess with just a couple of chairs placed strategically in warning, because he is due on gate duty. He sees the nursery children out of the side entrance in the rain, his hands white with diluted acrylic.

As the children leave, three contract cleaners arrive to vacuum and mop the offices and classrooms and clean the toilets. There have been problems with cleaners – mainly African and Eastern European immigrants ready to work for low wages and no job security – leaving early, skimping on the work, eating fish and chips in the classrooms so the smell lingers on the next morning. What John calls 'just people not playing the game, really'.

Looking after Edith Neville is not as onerous a job as it used to be. Before Seán found the money for the high railings around the outside, the school grounds were used by prostitutes working from King's Cross. 'It was ongoing at one point', says John. 'Needles and condoms all over the bushes, people still on site early in the mornings. When I asked them to leave, the men would run but the women would stroll off or threaten you.'

Since the fence was installed, the problems with intruders have reduced. Other issues persist however. The front of Edith Neville school looks out over a paved area landscaped with trees and dotted with clusters of smooth boulders. One of the few patches of Somers Town that offers space and privacy, it is used by carousing teenagers, lovers, drug dealers – addicts wait on the stones for men in cars who leave as quickly as they arrive – dog walkers and pram-pushing mothers, at different times of day. It is hardly overlooked – a rare commodity in an area where blocks of flats stand shoulder to shoulder – and functions off and on as an unofficial marketplace for stolen scooters and motorbikes, occasionally to the extent that parents are frightened to take their children out of the front gate of the school. Some of those involved in the trade are one-time Edith

Neville pupils, young men who were contained by primary school but whose lives fell apart at secondary, who have been in and out of the care system and special schools, boys without purpose who make trouble in disproportionate amounts for the residents of Somers Town.

Summers are the worst time for John Punton. When the flats are hot and the central London nights muggy, the area outside Edith Neville school comes alive. 'Kids gather on the rocks outside from midday to midnight and beyond', says John. 'Nicking bikes, skidding around, making a noise. There's vandalism, drug-takers, break-ins, motorbikes being set on fire, windows being smashed with airguns. You hear a bang. You try and switch off. But you can't. You know you're going to have to attend soon. It disrupts your evening.'

One of the pastimes of the gang members who gather on the boulders is throwing rocks at the windows of the school. The glass shatters inside the classrooms and goes everywhere. 'It gets in the kids' shoes', says John. 'It's an ongoing thing. You spend hours, clearing it, trying to make it safe.' He keeps sheets of wood at the ready, for boarding up windows. Once, he came into school to find fifteen broken. Since the two break-ins into Seán's office, metal shutters have been installed on his and Joan's office windows, where the confidential records are kept; they do not want children's details fluttering around the streets like confetti after a booze-fuelled break-in. The blinds are discreet though; no one wants the school to look like a fortress. Sometimes, they pull them down in the day against the sun.

* * *

Health and safety are causing ever more anxiety in schools, in a climate of compensation culture. Five-year-old KayLee, always accident-prone, swallowed a marble one afternoon. Before it had even worked its way out of the child's system, her mother was on the phone to the school threatening to sue. For some parents, winning the Lottery or suing the school are the only chances they see of ever making a substantial amount of money.

Heads around the country tell similar stories, of being threatened with litigation if a child falls over in the playground or trips in a corridor. Teachers can sue their schools as well; one brought an action after he slipped on a chip in the canteen. Many schools are curtailing activities to try to protect themselves from claims. They then find themselves pilloried for being over-cautious – as in the case of a Cotswolds primary that banned tinsel. A school in Carlisle in the north of England has started making children wear safety goggles if they want to play conkers. Other schools have banned parents from videoing school performances, or stopped taking children out of school on trips. In some cases, one safety imperative conflicts with another. The local government association was criticised by cancer charities after it advised teachers not to put sunscreen on children, in case they were accused of sexual or physical abuse.

Physical accidents – known in the insurance trade as 'trips and slips' – are just a part of what school governors can be held responsible for. In Walsall, a head teacher who gave a child a thirty-minute detention was accused by a solicitor of breaching the Human Rights Act. 'Failure to educate' is a growing area; in Hillingdon, in outer London, courts awarded a woman more than £45,000 because teachers at her former school failed to diagnose her dyslexia. Others have successfully sued local education authorities for failing to prevent bullying, for assaults, teacher stress and accidents on school trips. Manchester city council said it had received 158 claims for compensation over school accidents, costing more than £500,000, while in Hull costs regularly reach £300,000 a year. In Nottingham half of all claims for accidents during school hours were eventually dismissed.

The biggest cost to insurance companies from schools relates to school arson, rather than liability cases. Every year a handful of schools are burned down, often by former pupils. In 2003, fires in schools cost more than £73 million, according to Zurich Municipal, the largest insurers of schools and local education authorities. An average of twenty schools a week are damaged or destroyed by arson.

* * *

Schools are always in a state of flux; children join and leave, and the relentless rhythm of the school year pulls the community towards exams, festivals, half-terms and holidays. By the summer term, newly qualified teacher Lala Thorpe has left Edith Neville, in the middle of the school year and without another job to go to. Constant stage fright, anxieties about two boys who moved up from the two different nurseries – 'extreme behaviour and none of the adults knew how to manage it. It was horrific' – and guilt about her own children have combined to see her out of the profession. At home in her own kitchen in the first week of term, her bicycle propped in the hall, Lala feels nothing but relief about her decision. 'Teaching means giving up your life. It is not the sort of job you can do without giving it 100 per cent', she says. Her confidence never recovered from the shaky start she had, where beset by anxiety attacks she felt that the children saw through her and she was starring in an endless run of 'Faking It'.

Five-year-old KayLee left Edith Neville school at the same time, when her mother decided without warning to move her to a nearby church primary. Lala made a goodbye card for her to wish her well in her new school but KayLee's departure was as ragged as the rest of her life. A friend of her mother's came to collect her on the last day of term; KayLee hid under a table and refused to go with him. Lala had to get down on the floor and coax her out with sweets. 'These children stick in your mind for ever', she says. 'The training I had did not prepare me for behavioural issues or emotional neediness.'

Teacher Amy Crowther is back from her sabbatical in Australia, brown and thin, looking exotically different from when she went away. Her early years colleagues Laura O'Donoghue and Melanie Miah went to surprise her at Heathrow, Laura's shout of welcome echoing around Terminal Four, all three of them crying. Amy is taking over Lala's role as Reception teacher, leaving Isabel, the new teacher, to complete her qualifying year in Purple nursery undisturbed.

In the nursery, things are not going well for JoJo. He has reverted to mornings only after a series of angry episodes. Only Laura can manage him. She has been talking to the children about anger, and children have been reporting their own experiences of it. JoJo has told them about his dad getting angry, how he smashed his DVD player and then his mum fell down the stairs. Staff must try and read his behaviour for what it tells them about his life out of school.

Pierre's dad hit him outside the nursery, on the pavement, returning him after an access visit, when his son refused to say goodbye to him in the morning. Why couldn't he be happy like the other children, he shouted. Pierre's mum blamed the nursery staff for letting it happen. She came in the next day and shouted at Laura, threatened to take Pierre out of the nursery. Laura cups Pierre's face in her hands, smiles her 1000-watt smile. 'Beautiful boy', she says. 'My beautiful boy.'

Year 6, the oldest children in the school, are busy preparing for Sats tests in May. A number of them are in Collette's maths club first thing in the morning, working in twos and threes on problems she has set on a flipchart. Collette is success-making all round the room. 'Help Will! Don't tell him the answer, show him how to work it out.' 'Good try. Have you thought about doing it like this?' The children are morning-fresh, applying themselves to their maths, working on small white slates. At eight thirty, a message comes through from Jean Sussex: do they want beans or spaghetti?

In the music room, a stack of white toast is keeping hot in silver foil and the ketchup bottles are propped upside down. It is the end of the week and Jean and Yvonne have exhausted their supplies as they dish up scrambled egg and beans. 'Aidan! Here's your pepper!' Collette has breakfast with the children, hears about Will's holiday in Tenerife – and the maths goes on. If Collette was 13 when she went to Tenerife on holiday fifteen years ago – how old is she now? The girls have the answer in seconds flat.

Seán and Helen are still on the lookout for the brown envelope – which still has not come. The school has not been inspected for six years and is overdue for a visit from Ofsted. It is just chance that two of the strongest teachers – Nasima Rashid and Zoe Hamilton (now Lattimer) – have returned from their maternity leave, and Amy Crowther is back in Foundation stage. Had the inspectors called as expected to take their snapshot while these key players were away, they would not have seen the school at its strongest.

The day that began with maths club ends with a whole-school maths assembly, led by Seán. Children enter the hall to strains of *Così fan tutte* and arrange themselves in rows on the floor. Nursery children show their bar charts of how many of them like which kinds of fruit, Reception class display their shopping basket from nearby Chalton Street market, Year 2 represent odd and even numbers. Seán congratulates the mathematicians with delight – ‘my, you have been busy, bright and hardworking’ – and the first week of the summer term draws to a close.

NINE

BRIGHT BLUE, BEGINNING WITH T

Pauline: What is a shadow?
Fadil: A kind of twin brother.

'Good morning, Fiona', says nine-year-old Ahmed. 'I hope you have a fascinating day.' Each child in Fiona Gillespie's Year 4 class greets her, selecting their adjective from the list of forty or more on the board; she is wished in turn a blinding, amazing, captivating and awesome day. An extended vocabulary is a treasure Edith Neville children mainly do not have on arrival at school; Fiona is making sure they get a chance to acquire it.

After the grandiloquent greetings, she conducts a high-energy rush through the register, with a kitchen timer going. They make it in thirty-three seconds, which is not a record-breaker but good enough to send a sense of satisfaction through the room. The day begins with children feeling happy and successful; they are verbal sprinters, with good manners and a vocabulary worthy of the Oxford dictionary. The classroom is a place to have fun.

The room, decorated with children's self-portraits hanging from lines under the ceiling, is vibrant. There are times tables prominently displayed as well as the extended list of positive adjectives, artwork, environmental posters, children's stories and maths. Fiona's class are studying the fictitious Khan family, who live on the cyclone-prone island of Kukri Mukri in Bangladesh. The children gather on the carpet in front of her to recap on a recent assembly in which they explained to the whole school how the Khans eat breakfast of patna rice served with a sauce of garlic and chilli, sitting on mats outside their houses, how afterwards the men go fishing, the women grow fruits and vegetables in small plots of land. They go over why the houses are built on stilts – crop-haired Marcus waves his hand enthusiastically to supply the answer but when picked does not tell Fiona the reason; instead, he slaps himself on the head – and whether or not there is street lighting on the island.

Fiona brings out objects for a new classroom display. She has a painted wooden bangle holder, a palm leaf fan, lengths of bright, silky fabrics. A map of Bangladesh embroidered on sacking arouses real excitement. 'That's Dhaka', point out several children. 'Most of us are from Sylhet', another explains.

As the class breaks into groups at their tables to discuss the video 'The Eye of the Storm', produced by a British voluntary aid agency, a messenger arrives from the front office. 'Gozombor? Are you going to the dentist today? Have you got an uncle called Nahul? He is here for you.' Gozombor is not keen to leave, he is so involved in the geography lesson. 'Bangladesh is our real home', explains one child, who adds that she has never been there.

All the children seem focused and co-operative but there is a concentration of problems in this class. One child has severe learning difficulties, but no statement as yet and so no dedicated individual help. Another was recently abducted by a family member and remains traumatised. One is on the brink of being taken into care.

A recent arrival speaks no English at all. Two have emotional and behavioural difficulties.

One of these is Marcus, a tall boy with an open, intelligent face getting special attention from mentor Annabelle Ledford-Jobson. His feet in their large, brick-like trainers constantly move under the table. He lays one of them on its side, puts the other on top, reverses the position. His hands are constantly moving too, folding paper, putting things in and out of his pocket, taking the lid off and on his pen. Unthinking, he puts one knee up on the table and gets told off by Fiona. Marcus is now able to stay still for forty-five seconds, explains Annabelle, a considerable improvement on the fifteen seconds he could manage last year. But it is not enough to avoid trouble in the classroom. Before long, Marcus picks up a rolled straw mat, one of the Bangladeshi artefacts, and starts banging other children on the head with it at random. By morning break, he has been sent to Seán's office.

Marcus has already had his playtime cancelled for the whole week, after pushing a girl off the climbing frame. Being kept in at playtime – the vital outlet for the fidgety energy that seems mainly outside his control – is the worst thing for a child like him, says Annabelle. But the sanctions that would apply to any other child must apply to him too.

Annabelle, who works individually with twelve children in the school, aims to help children overcome barriers to achievement – in Marcus' case, his behaviour. He is quick and able but lacks powers of concentration and spends too much time getting into trouble. Mentors are funded by the government's Excellence in Cities programme, which aims to raise achievement in poor urban areas, particularly among children who have good academic potential but do not realise it, for social, emotional or practical reasons. Annabelle Ledford-Jobson radiates a form of honesty that enables her to tackle difficult issues with children and gain a well-placed trust from them. Good mentors can provide some of the cheerleading, problem-solving, individual attention that lucky children get a lot of at home.

* * *

In the early 1990s Ofsted, the schools inspection service, undertook a major study into why poor children fail at school. After visiting 134 schools in rundown urban areas, the inspectors reported that despite a general climate of school improvement, the most disadvantaged children were not benefiting. 'The rising tide of educational change is not lifting these boats', commented the authors of the study.

Ten years later, the problem 'is not solved', reported chief inspector David Bell after Ofsted revisited the subject in 2003. 'Progress in narrowing the gap in achievement has been slow', he admitted. The survey was bigger – this time investigating what was happening to children in 500 inner city primary schools and 70 secondary schools – but the results little changed. Bell provided a drily-expressed précis of the generally-recognised causes of the attainment gap, addressing a Fabian Society lecture. He was not talking specifically about Edith Neville's children but he might have been, since all the factors he identified apply in Somers Town to a greater or lesser degree.

'Many children from lower socio-economic groups, including large numbers of boys, suffer educational disadvantage because they lack well-informed parental support, financial backing, benign peer pressure and a healthy lifestyle', he said. 'These causes of disadvantage can be compounded by other factors, such as racial inequality, mobility or family disruption. Disadvantage shows itself in different guises but common to them are: low educational ambition; attitudes to learning which lack resolution and resilience; gaps in cultural knowledge relevant to the school curriculum; and weaknesses in useful academic skills, especially in language and independent learning.'

Inner city schools can and do raise children's attainment, but some appear better at it than others, said the chief inspector. 'Undoubtedly, there are schools that have succeeded against the odds: schools that were once in the doldrums and failing in every sense and yet have now been transformed into beacons of excellence and hope. We must continue to learn and apply the lessons from these most successful schools.'

It is no surprise that David Bell, who started his career as a primary school teacher and whose wife is a classroom assistant, said that the single most important factor in tackling educational disadvantage was better teaching. Schools serving marginalised communities, with the associated issues of poverty and disaffection in the classroom, are generally recognised to be the most challenging place to be a teacher. People working in them have to be not only on top of their subjects and methods but secure in themselves, to succeed. It helps too if children can recognise something of their own lives in the adults who stand in front of them.

* * *

Fiona Gillespie's high expectations of children are always in evidence, whether in the classroom or at an after-school club. More than twenty of the older children are waiting on benches in the school hall, to audition for the production of Snow White. 'But!' announces

Fiona in melodramatic style, 'it's a funny one.' Standing in front of them, in platform boots and dressed all in black, Fiona's is tough love. 'What is the c-word?' she asks the children, her words ringing into a pin-drop silence. All those who have ever been taught by her know the answer. 'Commitment!' they shout. Without that, she warns them, the production will fall apart.

Gozombor and Karim are vying for the part of narrator. Fiona sends them out into the lengthening shadows of the playground beyond the hall, to shout their chosen phrase – 'the big fat man dropped' – from five then ten then twenty metres. Two quiet girls go through the same procedure and find loud voices they never knew they had bellowing out of them in front of an audience. Marcus is a natural, auditioning as the wicked step-mother. He sneers and growls in front of an imaginary mirror, commanding the space at the front of the hall and calling for his huntsmen to bring him Snow White's heart in a box. 'And it ain't gonna be pumping', he informs his audience, with maximum menace. The children applaud and Fiona extends her hand. 'Put it there, Marcus.'

Fiona runs two drama clubs each week in Edith Neville, one before school and one after. As well as language, movement, self-confidence, literature, art and music it gives children, she says, 'a chance to go somewhere else and to be someone else'. This is something that she knows the value of. The oldest of six children, she comes from a background unfamiliar to most teachers – but all too well understood by some of Edith Neville's children. Her father was an alcoholic and the family constantly on the move. Starting life in Scotland, Fiona was enrolled in seven primary schools in as many years and by the age of eleven found herself in the south-west of England, where her mother had fled to a women's refuge. She arrived at secondary school, she says, neglected, insecure and aggressive. She became a champion table tennis player; sport gave her an outlet for her anger, the taste of success – and inspiration that she uses every day in Edith Neville school.

Fiona went back to college in her early twenties, acquired O and A levels and went on to train as a teacher. 'I never saw myself as an academic type,' she says, 'because of my background and roots. But I discovered that I could relate to children that were needy. I've got a natural ability to do that and to say to them "you can get out of this and become something and somebody". In a school where the children had no problems, I wouldn't be in my element.'

* * *

Teaching at Edith Neville is demanding. Teachers must be organised, energetic, passionate and inventive. All teachers need presence in the classroom – to attract the children's interest, and to be able to manage behaviour. The role demands stamina, self-belief and adaptability. People have to be team players – part of Edith Neville's success is due to the large number of different adults who work with children, whether as reading volunteers, bilingual or special needs assistants or classroom assistants. No one can expect to close the door and work alone. They have to be prepared to put in extra hours – running before- and after-school activities with the children, dealing with paperwork, getting involved in school environment projects or working in the holidays. They need to be well organised; space is at a premium and messy teachers are a liability.

Interestingly, deputy head Helen Griffiths says that the primary characteristic for a successful teacher at Edith Neville is that they be 'a listener'. 'Our ethos is about teaching children as individuals. You can't teach a child until you get to know them, not just as a person but as a reader, a writer, a scientist, a mathematician', she says. 'That involves listening to what they say, getting to know them as learners as well as making sure that their emotional and social needs are met.'

'A lot of people view teaching as filling empty vessels. I hope it isn't like that. Children have to develop themselves and as a teacher you don't know what's there until you start exploring – especially in a school like this where you might get children who have not been to school at all until the age of nine. Yes, we have got to deliver the National Curriculum. We do our job. But in a way that suits the children who are here.'

In an age of incessant government directives to schools, it takes confidence on the part of the head teacher and senior managers to foster teachers' autonomy and professional judgement. There is an unwritten law operating in education, whereby struggling schools must implement every directive from the government, Ofsted or the local education authority, whether or not they believe it suits their particular set of circumstances. But successful schools can plot their own course; if they are independent, innovative and at the top of the league tables, politicians and experts come looking for answers rather than seeking to impose them.

Edith Neville school is somewhere in the middle – successful enough to have won a degree of autonomy but not so well established as to be able to ignore the stream of bright ideas and initiatives that comes from Whitehall, even if they wanted to. Still, says Helen Griffiths, 'There are so many demands from government, we have to respond in a way that is not just a knee jerk reaction.'

* * *

All of Edith Neville's teachers bring a lot of themselves to the classroom. Nasima Rashid wanted to be a teacher from a young age. 'It was a romantic ideal,' she says, 'standing in front of the class, sharing books. That was my escape as a young girl, because we had a strict Muslim upbringing and were not allowed to go out and socialise.'

The A-level English that she had always wanted to study was a struggle. 'I was told I wasn't very good. I lacked a lot of the cultural knowledge around some of the texts. I didn't understand the references and the teachers didn't make it that accessible for me – which is why I always try to ground texts in children's knowledge.'

Her research at the Institute of Education (where she was studying for her Masters when she met Seán) crystallised her ideas about how children's learning is influenced by the expectations adults have of them. 'I came into it feeling I had to impart this knowledge to children, this sense that it's through education you will empower yourselves. I really believed that. I can empathise with some of the families', she says. 'I don't feel out of place. The difference was – my parents had this very strong belief that we had at least to be undergraduates.'

In school, children of Bangladeshi background used to think Nasima was English – until she spoke to them in their mother tongue. 'What really threw them was when I started speaking in Bengali, to prove I was Bangladeshi. I couldn't understand why they were surprised, because of the colour of my skin. But I realised they had seen very few people from the community speak English like I do. It came down to that. I made a conscious effort as a young person to make sure I spoke English in a way that didn't reflect my East End background. I think I was a bit of a snob.

'As a teacher, I've always been strict, with high expectations. That comes partly from my own upbringing – from my mother. And from my research in Tower Hamlets. I found that kids felt they came to school and played. They learned at the *madrasa* (Koranic schools run by mosques, in which children learn classical Arabic and study the Koran) and played at school. They respond well to clear boundaries and strict rules – things I'd observed in their Bengali and Arabic classes. They don't want the teacher as a friend – they need a clear role model. I have good relations with all the kids but especially the young Bengali girls. Seeing them quite demure and lacking in confidence and not getting the acknowledgement from home, I feel really fierce about grabbing them and saying "you can do it". I think I've made them respond well. It's a question of giving them confidence and self-belief.' When Nasima brought her sister, a doctor, into school it had a profound effect on the Year 6 Bangladeshi girls she was then teaching.

'Some of the Bengali children have read the Koran by the age of ten and I don't know how well that's recognised. We get bogged down with levels and targets. It's not just about trying to make them more like us. It's about knowing where they're starting from too.'

Nasima does talk about issues with the children – 9/11 and race riots in the north. 'But I don't want children to think this world is hostile. I want them to have some hope and confidence that they can move on.'

Several of the teachers and more than half the support staff at Edith Neville school are black or Asian. This does not go unnoticed locally. Bilingual assistant Rulie Naznin – a local resident and parent herself – says: 'The community likes this school, because there are more ethnic minority staff. They feel comfortable.'

* * *

The struggle for schools in the inner city is not just to find great teachers but to keep them. Collette Bambury is in her fourth year at Edith Neville and taking Year 6 into their tests. Committed and highly effective, there is a sense in Collette's classroom that no child risks losing their dignity. She too has wanted to be a teacher since childhood – when she used to go into her own school in the holidays to help her mother, who worked as a dinner lady, get things ready for term. She 'immediately clicked' with Helen Griffiths when she came for interview, she says, and enjoys the challenge of Edith Neville. 'I feel I can deal with behaviour OK. I was a bit naughty at school myself and if the lessons were boring I might start misbehaving. So I know what to watch out for.' What will push Collette out of the inner city is not children being naughty but the price of flats; she and her boyfriend want to buy their own place. 'Money is the reason I'll probably end up leaving London, because it is so expensive. The way to get more money is to become a manager. But the only thing I like doing is the teaching.'

Amy Crowther left London wanting a 'clean, clear break'. Although she had agreed with Seán that she would take a sabbatical, even by the day she left school she was not sure in her own mind about whether she would come back to Edith Neville. Exhausted by acting up in the absence of other senior staff, by the prospect of Ofsted and by the break-up of her relationship, she left for Australia and threw herself into learning to sail. 'I really got into it', she says. 'It felt quite alien, when people were emailing me telling me stories from work.'

While there, she got a temporary job in a nursery in Sydney – which convinced her to come back to Somers Town. 'It made me realise how much I enjoyed working at our school', she says. 'It was a fantastic school, with a similar intake, but there just wasn't the same sense of commitment, from the staff to the children. They didn't spend the time talking to the children about issues.'

She decided to come back to London, rejoin Edith Neville, support her colleagues through the inspection – and took up Seán's suggestion that she team teach in Reception with newly qualified Gina. 'A lot of people said I should move on, get a new challenge', she says. 'But I'm happy here. I don't want to take on another massive challenge just yet.' Amy wants to keep on working with children. Her future plans include working in a children's centre. She has a new responsibility post at Edith Neville – as school and community co-ordinator, to build up work with parents and the community, an area she feels strongly about.

Amy Crowther, at 29, is still in touch with her first primary teacher. She had an 'idyllic time' at school, she says, in a class of seven with people she is still friends with. It is this, more than anything, that makes her the teacher she is.

* * *

Most of the children in Edith Neville school have English as a second language; while this may in the long run be positive for the children, the extra issues it poses in primary school are huge. When supply teacher Dora asks Year 1 for a word meaning 'see-through, like a window', only Harry – one of two native English speakers in the class – can supply the answer 'transparent'. When later, playing a word game, she wants a 'kind of bright blue that begins with t', nobody knows turquoise. What happens to my skin in the sun? she says, holding out her hand. 'Sun town', suggests one child, valiantly. 'Tan', Harry corrects him. Yet the majority of the children in the class have already outstripped their parents' command of English.

David Bell identified 'gaps in cultural knowledge relevant to the curriculum' as one of the hallmarks of educational disadvantage. This does not only mean lack of expertise on grand themes like the British political system or history. In Year 1, only a couple of children are familiar with the idea of a cat flap, on which their story today – the continuing adventures of the cat Slinky Malinki – is based. Dora holds up a picture of Slinky Malinki asleep on a hearth rug between two floral couches, in front of an open fire. Can the children 'read' the image as a cosy home? Or does it look like a barn on fire, with its leaping flames and sleeping animals?

Half a dozen children leave the room for their reading recovery programme. It is possible to be well behind by the age of six. Dora continues with the story, putting in plenty of expression, drawing responses out of the children, about the darkness, what makes light at night, why they know that this is a bad cat and that a good one. (By the yellow eyes.)

Nasima Rashid believes that having English as an additional language can benefit children – but only if staff have an understanding of bilingualism. 'It is important to have that awareness, and build it into pedagogy', she says. At Foundation stage, it is easier. There are bilingual assistants in the nursery and Reception classes, books to be read in other languages, by native speakers. But as children's learning becomes more formalised as they move up through the school, the opportunities to acknowledge the language and culture they inhabit at home become more rare.

Basic language skills take between two and five years to acquire. More advanced ones up to seven years. But, says Nasima, 'we haven't got space to allow that language development'. Even she, who went through it herself, finds it hard to be mindful sometimes, she says, of the children's particular requirements. The curriculum and national tests make no allowance for children still learning English, apart from giving a little extra time in tests. For EAL learners, says Nasima, 'you need to be really explicit, revisit things, breaks things down' – what she calls 'chunking'. 'All good teachers do that. But in our environment, it's more important.'

* * *

After school on Thursdays, Suad runs Somali club in the parents' room that doubles as music room and breakfast club room. Eight children sit round a long table, each with a carton of milk and a lined exercise book in front of them. Mainly aged around 8 and 9, there are five girls and three fidgeting, table-pushing boys. All come from homes where Somali is spoken, although to each other they speak English. Suad, standing at the top of the table while a summer rain lashes down outside, speaks to them entirely in Somali. She is elegant in yellow-gold ear-rings, a long-sleeved top and skirt, with henna on her fingertips, effortlessly modelling to the children that you can live and work successfully in England without relinquishing a Somali identity.

After reading a story (*sheeko*) about a grandmother (*ayeeyo*), Suad talks to the children about relatives they have back in Somalia. One of the girls reports that she has two grandmothers in Somalia, one aged 50 and one aged 58. Suad asks the children in Somali about other relatives in Somalia, if they were born there, if they have ever been to visit, or have plans to visit. Some of the children are uncertain, when speaking in their parents' tongue. But Suad says they are less reluctant to speak Somali than they were when she began the club a couple of years before. Several are going to Somalia this summer and she encourages them to send postcards, take photographs, write a diary while they are there.

Some of the Bengali-speaking bilingual assistants run a similar club for children of Bangladeshi heritage. The school invests in these clubs – the staff are paid overtime to run them – because they consider it important that children's cultural and linguistic heritage is seen to be valued by the school, part of their learning rather than an impediment to it. It is an extra, unrecognised job for the school – not just to immerse children in English language and culture but also to uphold their language and culture of origin.

The girls gather up the pencils, scissors, glue and exercise books and before they go home Suad reads to them. Today's story – 'The Musicians of Bremen' – owes nothing to Somali culture. Bur she reads it from a Somali language book, asks questions in Somali. 'Otherwise', she says, 'they keep talking English all the time.' She has Somali books; their stories feature adventurous boys, leopards, monkeys, mosques, moral tales of bravery, cowardice and wit. Most Somali parents, says Suad, are keen that their children keep up the language and learn to read it. Some of the children complain that it sounds like shouting. She tells them: 'It is not shouting. It is strong.'

TEN

IN THE BLACK

'Get rid of stinging nettles in the playground. Seats on the grass. Colour printers. Help with our reading. Meet a real MP.'
Edith Neville's school council wish list

In Purple nursery, Ali is crying uncontrollably. His mother is twenty-five minutes late to collect him, and all the other children are long gone. Laura sits on the carpet, attempting to interest him in the wooden train set for which there is usually fierce competition among the boys. Ali, breath heaving, is inconsolable. When the mother comes, Laura tells her off, because she is often late both to drop him and to collect him. 'You must try and come on time, mummy', she says, with her customary good humour. 'It's not good for Ali, to be upset like this.' 'Mummy' ignores her, smiling at her son. 'Did you think I'd left you here? I wouldn't leave you.'

Laura and Francisca mutter, when she has gone. 'We're too soft with them', says Laura. 'If this was a church school, we wouldn't put up with it. We're not social services.' After a draining day, they now have no time for a coffee before parents' evening begins at four o'clock. They will start taking Ali to wait in the office when the mother is late, they decide, to make the point more clearly. Staff at Edith Neville have been known to stay on till six o'clock, waiting for parents. The alternative – taking children to the police station or to social services – is a last resort.

It is newly qualified Francisca's first parents' evening and her nerves are not helped by the fact that Seán and Nasima are amongst those who have booked an appointment to come and talk about their child. Bilingual assistant Shavi stands by for translations into Bengali. Sultan has settled well, Francisca tells his mother, after a slightly difficult start. Mother is worried about his maths. Francisca is worried about his attendance.

The next mother complains that her son loves the books he brings home from nursery. 'He makes me read it and read it', she says. 'I haven't got time.' Laura is forthright. 'You've got to make time, mummy.' Laura can say things to parents that teachers can't say. She peppers her remarks with a smattering of Bengali – *balla, balla*, she says (good). *Aste, aste* (quickly). Where's *abba*? (father).

Fourteen of the twenty-six children's parents come to see staff, over the course of three evenings. Several of the parents report that their children cry at the weekends, because there is no nursery. Pierre's mother does not come, nor his father. Najreen's mother makes an appointment, but does not keep it. JoJo's mother comes, slipping in on time for her slot. Laura and Francisca are able to report some progress. 'He's not going under the table at dinner time', they tell her. 'He paints, and cuts, and sticks. He asks for help.' Although still troubled, JoJo seems to be responding to the calm and consistent management of his behaviour, and the encouragement and love staff show him. Nicki has noticed a change at home as well. 'He is starting to cry when he is upset, instead of hitting things', she says.

* * *

'Our job is to improve the life chances of the children in our care. That is what we are engaged in, every day.' Teachers, nursery nurses and assistants are all crowded into a classroom, sitting round the low tables like proxy children while deputy head Helen Griffiths reminds them of the vision. 'Never mind what Ofsted is telling us to do, and the local education authority, and the Department for Education. We all came to this school to make a difference to children here, in Somers Town. So what do we want in the year ahead?'

The staff recap on what has been positive about the year gone by. Sports, the summer fair, Sats results, trips out, assemblies, clubs, refugee week, new staff, parents' groups, interactive whiteboards, fresh flowers in reception are all mentioned. They brainstorm on what they would like to happen next year and come up with a wide-ranging – and budget-busting – list. More non-contact time, they decide, in which to plan and assess. New computers, laptops and printers. More clubs, games to play at lunchtimes. A chill-out room for children. Better dinners, toilets, drinking fountains.

Helen is in charge of the school improvement plan, a detailed document of ideas about how to make the school better, in major and minor ways – and a legal requirement. She will be feeding staff views back to the governing body and as a governor herself is well aware of the financial constraints on their activities. She tells everyone that to avoid feeling demoralised, overloaded and unsupported by colleagues, it is best to consider what changes they can effect themselves – 'so we're not setting ourselves up for failure'.

Amy's table look again at the item on top of their wish list, more money for trips. Trips don't have to cost money, they decide. The children generally lack outdoor experience, so even going to the shops or the park can be beneficial. They are already planning a trip to Princess Diana's memorial fountain in Hyde Park; that does not cost anything. They can use the underground for free. They begin to discuss making a booklet of ideas of things for parents to do with their children at the weekends.

'We recognise that we are a good school', Helen tells everyone, seriously. 'What we are involved with now is inching forward. And that is the hard bit.' Helen speaks with authority and confidence; she has a secure grasp of both the vision and the detail. Since last year, she has gone through the training necessary for all new head teachers – getting the National Professional Qualification for Headship on a fast track. She is clearly head teacher material and would have no trouble getting a post.

But still she hesitates. 'I'm not ready, psychologically', she says, later. 'I just don't know if I want to be the one who is carrying the can.' She is wearing an engagement ring, getting married in the summer holidays. 'It's not the wedding that's exciting', she says. 'It's the man. He's the bee's knees.'

* * *

Governors meet once a term for a full governing body meeting, in the music room, over custard creams and orange juice. Smaller committees then take up work in specific areas. Seán has served for twelve years on the governing body but keeps a low profile. The atmosphere is friendly, serious and to a degree formal. Among staff and governors at Edith Neville, there are plenty of ideas about how to improve the school further, plenty of will and motivation – but insufficient money to carry out many of the plans.

When Helen brings the school improvement plan to a governing body meeting, of the scores of items for action the ones on which there has been absolutely no progress are without exception the ones which cost money – improving drinking water provision, for instance, and ICT infrastructure, finishing off the fence around the school, creating an adequate library.

The school year at Edith Neville begins in April, but despite government promises to introduce three-year budgets, at this point governors still do not know how much money they will be getting. On top of which, Edith Neville's budget has shrunk, to just over £1 million per school year. The loss of £60,000 in urban regeneration grants has hit hard. A grant to support the achievement of children from ethnic minorities has been frozen although wages have not, meaning a net loss of extra help in real terms.

Most of the money goes on salaries. The governors invest heavily in staff training and development – this both improves the quality of people's work and helps keep them in the school, because it means they are growing professionally. 'The success of the school depends on the quality of the staff and the level of support we can offer', says chair of governors John Twigg. 'But our ability to deliver it is being slowly but surely eroded.'

Erratic and shrinking budgets make it very difficult to plan ahead. 'It runs completely counter to the Department for Education's view that governors should be in charge of the strategic vision of the school', says John. 'You need to know that you are going to be able to have teaching assistants, bilingual assistants, not just this year but next year and the years after that.'

Schools are run by something like a jury – a collection of people who together are seen to be greater than the sum of their parts. Composition varies in different areas but always includes parent governors, teacher governors, and representatives from the local education authority and the community. 'It is difficult to explain what governors actually do', remarks Edith Neville's chair of governors John Twigg. 'Because we're not always terribly sure.' This should not be taken to indicate any lack of competence on the part of John Twigg – the 47-year-old, socially minded academic and father of two children at the school is highly thought of and seen as both conscientious and effective.

Without mandatory training or, necessarily, any knowledge of education, school governors are meant to be able to take responsibility for all major decisions affecting school life. They must also respond to the ever-changing dictates from government. Politicians determine what should happen and governors scramble behind with practical arrangements.

John Twigg believes training after election to the governing body should be a condition of entry to the role. The skills people bring, he says, are a lottery. 'There is a basic issue about how you prepare people to be governors. What are your responsibilities? Your tasks? If you went into a job, you would have a clear specification. The broad goals are there, but the advice from the Department for Education is nebulous.'

There is, says John Twigg, a culture of consensus on Edith Neville's seventeen-strong governing body – 'a desire to arrive at decisions everyone can sign up to'. This is not always the case. When the head and the chair cannot agree – not an issue at Edith Neville – the smooth running of the school is effectively halted until one or both depart.

Party politics are supposed to be left at the door when governing bodies meet; there has been consternation over the election to school governing bodies of far-right activists in the British National Party, in Calderdale in Yorkshire and in the West Country. A more common problem – and one in evidence at Edith Neville – is recruiting enough, representative local parent and community governors. The responsibilities are heavy for conscientious school governors and the work must be done for its own sake. Edith Neville has introduced mentoring and an induction pack for new governors and a guide to the hundreds of acronyms via which school life is navigated.

Self-employed John Twigg, who describes himself as a 'jobbing writer, consultant and researcher for international aid agencies', says he could not fulfil the role if he had a full-time job. Vice chair of governors Esther Caplin is also self-employed. 'We can shape our lives a bit around the responsibilities', says John. Governors too are subject to Ofsted, and can be held to account for not fulfilling their role as 'critical friend'. They also wait with some anxiety for the brown envelope – which has still failed to materialise. 'There has been a steady improvement in standards', says John. 'The concern is how to maintain it and how to make strategic plans in the context of the political winds blowing from Whitehall.'

ELEVEN

STRAWBERRY ICE-CREAM

'You can't judge a girl by her T-shirt'
Slogan on Ellie's top

Year 6 teacher Collette Bambury has arranged a special evening for parents and children to come and get their test results from her in person. Most families don't turn up but Roberto comes with his mum and dad and the youngest of his many brothers. Tall and heavily built, Roberto has an animated, shining face and gentle manner. The affection between him and his teacher is evident. Roberto's family are from Namibia; his parents are supportive of all their sons' education and regularly attend parents' evenings and other meetings.

Roberto has got a level 4 for English, meeting the national expected standard for his age. And a level 5 – better than average – for maths. 'You've done absolutely brilliantly, Roberto', Collette says. 'We're very proud of you – put it there.' Roberto looks pleased as he holds out his hand, but quickly returns to a subdued state. He had hoped for a level 5 for science as well as maths and in class Collette had assessed him as working at level 5. On the day, in the test, he was a couple of marks short and got a level 4. He seems to feel he has failed.

Collette praises his hard work, sportsmanship and popularity in the class. He has played netball for Camden and takes a leading role in the forthcoming Year 6 show. For coming to school, Roberto has scored 100 per cent, another rare achievement in Somers Town. 'His attendance has been excellent, which really helps', she tells his parents, mindful perhaps of the younger boys coming along. Mum does not hear; she has already left the classroom, chasing after her newly-walking toddler.

Roberto might be seen as a textbook example of the idea that if parents support their children, communicate with the school, and have high aspirations for them they will do well, whatever their home circumstances or cultural background. Roberto is a black boy in the inner city; he comes from a cramped home in which no adult is a native English speaker and money is in short supply but belief in education is strong. He seems likely to continue to do very well at school.

In fact, all the Year 6 children at Edith Neville have done exceptionally well this year, exceeding the national average in their test results. Most startling are the results in English. Of the twenty-seven children in the class, three-quarters speak English as a second language. Yet the published results will indicate that 82 per cent got level 4 or above in English – 'phenomenal for our school', says Nasima. Four of the five children who reached level 5 in English were Bangladeshi girls. 'Bright, hardworking girls', says Nasima. 'If you think about where they started, when they came into nursery with no English really, it is amazing. If you have high expectations, they will rise to it.'

In maths – easier than English for speakers of English as an additional language – the score is in the mid-nineties for those achieving level 4 or above. In fact, only one child taking the test did not reach level 4. Eleven got level 5. One child got a level 6. In science too, only one child did not reach a level 4; she has just been awarded a statement for her severe learning difficulties.

'I should retire now', Seán throws over his shoulder, as he runs his finger down the yellow carbon list of names and numbers. He means that the results are more likely to go down than up next year, because of the characteristics of the year group. But when a school slips in the league tables, the general interpretation is that that school is getting worse.

Collette Bambury's hopes for the children she has taught for two years are not measurable in tables. 'I just hope they're all going to be really happy,' she says, 'whatever their decisions are. They are happy now, so you just want them to stay happy.'

* * *

The Sats are over but the drive to give children all possible knowledge, skills and experience to launch them on their secondary careers continues. In the children's last few weeks at Edith Neville, Year 6 takes on the air of an inner city finishing school, with teacher Collette taking her class out for as many new and rich experiences as she can cram in before they are gone, compensating in part for the narrow focus on English, maths and science that is necessary in all schools in the weeks before Sats.

The local community police officer visits to warn of the dangers of involvement with the street gangs that are much in evidence in

Somers Town. Word has reached the staff that some of the older children are already hanging around the edges of the gangs; some play out on the streets till late at night while others are still barely allowed to leave their flats. 'It is a dangerous area to be living in at their age', says Collette.

Learning mentor Annabelle holds circle times to work on children's feelings about the transfer to secondary school. She gets the children into the hall, asks them to position themselves in one of three areas under the wall bars depending on whether they are 'really, really, ready' for the change, 'more or less ready' – or 'terrified'. Most put themselves in the first spot, none in the third; three months previously, almost all had been 'terrified'. 'You should all be proud because every single one of you has made progress in how you feel', she tells them. This emotional work, vital preparation for the challenges of secondary transfer, is considered important at Edith Neville.

Annabelle moves them on to role-playing in pairs – pretending one has been wrongly accused of either fighting or stealing and the other child is sticking up for them as their friend. All the children are now fluent in English – and most are willing to speak in front of their peers. 'She's a very sensible and mature person, it cannot be', says Zubeda, on being called by an imaginary secondary school teacher to act as a character witness for Salma. 'Use your friendships as a strength when you are in trouble', Annabelle counsels. 'Try not to keep things all to yourself.' 'It's our last Wednesday ever', Rory realises, aloud.

Later in the day, school nurse Anne Bunko comes in to talk more about relationships. She stands in front of Year 6, trying to get the VCR working. 'The video we are about to watch shows you a little bit about how you have sex, what sort of things need to come together', she says, distractedly. One of the children comes forward to make the tape run. 'While you're watching, I want you to think about how you choose your friends.'

The children are tall, most some distance into puberty. Their feet are large, their legs long and faces lengthening almost visibly. All the girls wear trousers; as yet, only one covers her hair. Sporty Salma is star of the netball and girls' football teams; her traditionally minded Muslim parents want her to give up sport now her periods have started. Some of the girls are experimenting with make-up, wearing glittering ear-rings; some of the boys look equally image-conscious, with hair gel and huge undone trainers.

The video, 'Living and Growing; how babies are made', is a mixture of relationships and biology. A line-drawn couple having energetic intercourse prompts laughter among the class. Collette puts the tape on pause and speaks sternly. 'I've been horrified to know how many of you have seen 18-rated films at home. You've probably seen it with real adults. You need to pay attention to this because when you get to secondary school you might hear things that are wrong, from other children.' Year 6 watches the rest of the video straight-faced.

When Anne Bunko takes the floor again, tough boy Craig wants to talk about love at first sight. One girl wants to know if parents can have the same understanding of a child they adopt, as one they give birth to themselves. Another asks whether a menstruating woman must wash with hot water if there is a man in the house. The pupils have had the opportunity earlier to put questions in a box, anonymously. Some are inventive: 'what happens if sperm get stuck together?' Some daring: 'what are sex toys and how do you use them?' But all get the same straight response. 'The most common thing is something called a vibrator. The woman can use it to sort of tickle herself inside.' Anne's unembarrassable stance makes for calm discussions of erections, labour, designer babies. 'You might find in Year 7 and 8, it never gets talked about again', she says.

Most parents, serial surveys find, think sex education should be up to teachers. But not all teachers are comfortable with talking about intimate matters with children. 'Some parents haven't actually talked about sex at all to the children and some staff say they find it quite difficult too', says Anne Bunko. 'You need to begin pre-school, talking very naturally about things as they arise. Children watch MTV – but their parents won't talk to them normally about sex. Children pick up on the double standards.'

Edith Neville encourages families to let their children attend the sex education classes at school; while some have needed persuasion to co-operate, currently only one Muslim father is exercising his legal right to withdraw his three children from sex education.

* * *

Ostensibly, parents in Somers Town can choose which secondary school their children go to. In reality, few parents here have any choice of secondary schools. Those with children with statements of special educational needs can have free choice. Others can apply to any school, but unless it is the local school are unlikely to win places. The popular schools in the richer north of the borough fill up with the siblings of children already there, and then the children living closest to them. Every year, Seán holds a meeting to talk to parents about secondary transfer and warns against 'aspirational and unrealistic choices'. Every year, some parents continue against the odds, to have aspirations that their children should go to the favoured schools rather than the ones nearest at hand. One mother of a child from another primary school in the borough chained herself to the railings outside Camden Town Hall, after failing to get a place for her daughter at one of the more popular schools.

When secretary of state for education, Charles Clarke lamented the fact that for 'far too many London parents the choice is between long journeys or going private'. For far more, he might have added, neither of these is an option. Eleven-year-old Rima is leaving Edith Neville after seven years in the school. Her mother, who came to England from Morocco, is anxious about her daughter's move to secondary school. 'At the moment, Rima respects everybody and if she stays like this, I'll be really happy. I say to her "if you change – I swear I'll take you on a one-way ticket to Morocco".'

Leyla left school herself aged ten. But that doesn't mean she is not passionately concerned about her daughter's education. She wanted her to go to the local school, on the grounds that it is closest to home. Rima, who was one of the children to get a level 5 in her science test, hopes to be a doctor. Like many children, her immediate aspiration for secondary transfer is to be safe. She has heard scare stories about her local secondary. 'All the Asian people fight with all the English people. They tied one boy to the bike rack and beat his head with a hammer', she says. She had also been bullied by some of the older girls there. She rejected that option.

Then, Leyla began her research campaign. Every day, after dropping off her two daughters at Edith Neville, she took a thermos of coffee and got a bus to the north of the borough, to stake out secondary schools. She runs through their qualities, as viewed from the main road. 'Skirts up to here', she gestures at her chin. 'No way. They look as if they are going to the disco.' The convent? 'Drinking lager outside the gates, and swearing.' She had thought she wanted a small school for Rima. But in the end it was a large, all-girls, school that won her approval. 'The girls are like English people sixty years ago. No short skirts, no high heels, no showing the body. Like old ladies.'

They applied for a place at their school of choice. But Rima was 182nd on the waiting list. They appealed, and on the grounds that both her parents have disabilities, Rima was jumped to the top of the list. It is a quest that few succeed in.

Rima is reassured by her visit to her new school – 'tidy and it smells of air freshener', she says. She has different ideas from her mother. As Leyla recalls how children in Morocco would be beaten on the feet for coming late to school, Rima brings her gently back to earth. 'You can't beat people for being late, mummy. What if they're stuck in the lifts?'

Collette hopes that most of the Year 6 children will go on to college after secondary school, although university attendance is low amongst Bangladeshi women in particular and children from poor backgrounds in general in Britain. Year 6 have ambitions to be doctors, lawyers and teachers. Edith Neville has helped them believe that they can be these things – while recognising that some of the girls will almost certainly go on to early arranged marriages, or not be allowed by their parents to go to university. 'You have got to be very delicate, but show them different life experiences', says Collette. 'I don't know how their lives will unfold but I do know that they won't be playing catch-up at secondary school.'

* * *

Six coaches pull away from outside Edith Neville school, leaving a thin line of mothers waving from the pavement, scarves caught by the breeze. The nursery staff are laden with bags full of children's packed lunches, buckets and spades from Purple nursery's sandpit, loo rolls, sick bags, towels, sunscreen, money collected for ice-creams, school mobile phones, lists of children allowed and not allowed to paddle. Laura is already there in her head – 'we can see seaweed, and shells', she tells the nursery children, sounding thrilled. 'Make sandcastles.' JoJo is dressed up in a new short-sleeved shirt and matching trousers, with his picnic in his rucksack; he cried when all the other children went to join their parents in the hall – he is one of five nursery children who are not accompanied by a parent. As the coach lurches past Hawksmoor's Spitalfields church a few miles east of the school, the first child is sick.

Every year, the school puts on a whole-school outing to Broadstairs. Every year, there are some children and parents in the party who have never seen the sea. The outing is a focal point for the dog days of the summer term and a way of promoting the sense of school as family, as a community of people who can adopt different roles with each other in a different context. Parents are encouraged to come, all the staff come (apart from caretaker John Punton, who remains behind to guard the fort), and only a few Year 6 children opt out, on the grounds that they are 'bored of Broadstairs'. The early years children have been anticipating the trip for weeks. As the coach enters Thanet, a silvery stretch of water comes into view on the horizon and the air fills with shouts of 'we can see the sea'.

It starts to rain just as the party arrives at the beach. Adults and children rush for shelter in a covered pub-garden at sand-level. Roberto's mum is there with the baby tied into a patterned cloth on her back, and Hibo, her picnic packed into a large striped bag and her feet sandy. Crowded into the dank concrete space, JoJo eats part of his jam sandwich and opens a paper bag containing, to his delight, two wagon wheel biscuits. The sand, patterned with gull prints, is ginger-coloured under a stormy sky; Seán is out on it, alternately chasing and being chased by a Year 6 boy with a watergun. Yesterday, he was giving an assembly dressed in traditional Bengali costume of long kirta and loose trousers. Today, he looks equally unfamiliar, in a T-shirt and khakis. Jean Sussex is dressed up for the day – in a nautical-looking striped top. Immaculate twin sister Joan is dressed down – in trousers.

A short break in the rain gets the school out of the shelter and onto Broadstairs's horseshoe-shaped bay. Amy follows Pierre as he plunges fully clothed into the waves; JoJo goes into the shallows and emerges holding a starfish by one point, eyes wide; Najreen cowers as a gull nearly as big as she is stretches its wings out next to her on the sand. The rain falls again, sudden and heavy, soaking the trays of chips in paper bags, the children's hair, the spread picnic rugs. JoJo shivers uncontrollably. His spare clothes were used on the coach on the way down, after the boy in the next seat was sick over him. The strap on his rucksack has broken, his socks and trousers are soaked. He eats a carton of strawberry ice-cream in a café high above the beach, jumping up between mouthfuls to jab at the buttons on the fruit machine.

The atmosphere on the way home in the coaches is subdued. Just before departure, two mothers had a fight on the beach. Amy got hit on the head when she intervened. Many of the children saw the fight, which sprang from an earlier disagreement between the two women's children. The trip was rushed, the time between rains too chopped up to allow the children to settle to playing, and the tussle on the sand seems to have brought on a sense of collective shame. Amy and Mel don't use the word disappointed but their laughter on the way back has a manic edge to it; they hate to see the children short-changed. It seems as if the party somehow brought the inner city with it, could not, in the end, leave it behind. For the first time any-one can remember, the group gets back early to school. It is also, announces Jean Sussex, the first time in twenty years that it has rained when Edith Neville have gone to Broadstairs.

Laura's sunny outlook remains unaffected. 'Home again', she says, looking with satisfaction as the grimy Caledonian Road – known locally as Cally Road – unfolds through the window of the coach, pointing out her own primary school to the children. 'I'm a Cally girl.' Francisca, sitting in front of her, smiles.

TWELVE

PINK HEARTS

'You go home thinking about them and you wake up thinking about them.'
Teacher Collette Bambury, on her Year 6 class

It is the last day of the summer term. 'Day 190 for the children, day 194 for us', says Seán, in morning briefing. He congratulates newly qualified teachers Francisca Fung and Nick Russell on getting through their first year – and winning qualified teacher status – and warns of the need to keep children calm in the leavers' assembly. 'We wouldn't want the high levels of emotion to result in behaviour that would sully their last day', he says. The boiler is malfunctioning and despite the bright sunshine outside the radiators cannot be switched off. Jean fans herself with the day's itinerary, sweating slightly.

* * *

A mum has brought her child, due to start next term, for a visit to Purple nursery. Pale and wan, he sits drinking milk on her lap. JoJo arrives half an hour late. He looks well, bright-eyed and with glossy hair. His long eyelashes flicker; he is still not wearing his glasses. He smiles at Laura, goes straight to the paper and paints table and starts to draw around the outside of his left hand.

The atmosphere in the nursery is ragged and scattered; staff, who still have a lot of packing and sorting to do, want the children outside in the sunshine for a run around. JoJo, with a red felt pen in his hand, is not interested in going outside. While the others play on the climbing frame and the scooters, he continues to work on his own at the table by the staffroom door. He is colouring shapes he has cut out, from a stencil. 'Look', he holds it up, looking round for someone to show. 'I'm drawing it.'

He is still engrossed much later, when the children come in for a story and Laura tells him to join the others on the carpet. 'JoJo', she says, when he makes no response. 'I'm going to count to three.' He hastily puts the lid on the pen and jumps out of the chair to sit on the carpet. 'Good listening, JoJo', Laura says.

* * *

Seán still awaits the brown envelope as the school year draws to a close. Ofsted 'in abeyance' is not particularly helpful to the smooth running of the school, he says. 'It is fully three calendar years I've been expecting a letter. It is an unhealthy distraction. You cannot keep up that level of adrenalin.'

Waiting for Ofsted has also had practical implications for the school. Teachers were kept with difficult classes two years running

– because they were managing them well and, with several key staff absent in the expected Ofsted visit period, Seán needed all the help he could get. It has held him back from self-development, he says. He has trained as an inspector and might have done a couple of inspections himself – earning some much-needed money for the school and giving colleagues the opportunity to act up. If he was planning to apply for another headship – which he is not – that too would have to wait until post-Ofsted. The local education authority have dangled various opportunities in front of him, including headships of larger schools, and an advisory post – which might allow him more time to spend with his own children – but so far nothing has tempted him sufficiently.

Seán has decisions to make after the inspectors finally do come. Promoted while still very young, he has been head of Edith Neville for over six years already and is not yet 40. The question of how long he can do the job is unavoidable. He and Nasima have two young children and are keenly aware of their responsibilities to them too. 'The basic model for successful heads is predicated on having no life and just working all hours', he says. 'And I'm perpetuating it.'

He went to the GP about his insomnia; the doctor advised him to take a 'drug holiday' from school – just as he has advised the other five head teachers on his books to do. Seán went into the surgery with no intention of taking medication, but walked out with a prescription for a sleeping pill.

Seán has twice as many applications as places for Reception next year. The catchment area is down to 0.185 of a mile. Several of the children in the two nurseries have not got places in the Reception class; parents have been coming in tears to beg. Among the new intake is a child who is life-threateningly allergic to a number of everyday foods; Amy, Mel and others have had training in giving the emergency injection in case of an attack.

Seán and Nasima were looking forward to their summer holiday but Seán's father has been taken ill, throwing their plans into the air. Of the six-week summer holiday, Seán will take about three weeks; the rest of the time will be spent at school catching up on what went undone this year and readying things for the next. The budget just does not allow for the non-teaching deputy and extra administrative support that the school needs.

Seán, recognised as a successful and experienced head, says he still finds the job very hard. 'Even with the warmth and support of most of the adults and, I think, all of the children.'

* * *

Children file into the hall for the Year 6 leavers' assembly, older children making more rows behind the younger ones until the whole school is assembled with the nursery classes right at the front. Maharun sits, in a summer dress, on Sue Garrett's lap. The hall has a festive air – the wall bars are hung with a giant Romeo and Juliet banner, in silver letters on a purple background, decorated with pink hearts. Another banner depicts a starry sky and on the wall opposite is a third, bearing the words 'Love is in the air', all made by Year 6.

About thirty parents have come, one with a video camera, and the air is alive with adult chat. Sue Garrett orientates Maharun, tells her who is sitting on either side of her, and where the stage is. With everyone assembled, Seán – dressed once again in his dark suit – takes the floor. 'Good morning, Seán', chorus the children. Seán 'celebrates a great year'. Many children's work is better, friendships are stronger, lives are happier, he tells the assembled school. It is also a sad day, he tells them, because 'there has to come a time when we say goodbye'.

Year 6 enter the hall with jaw-dropping effect. Overnight, Craig has peroxided his hair. This combines with his Asian features and skin to make a stunning Romeo. No child is elevated above another in this graduation performance. All the boys are Romeo – in leather or denim jackets, and shades, shuffling, strolling or strutting. And all the girls are Juliet, some made up and bejewelled, some unadorned according to their personal interpretation of young womanhood. Teacher Collette sits in the audience on the floor, among the nursery children, tissue in hand as Year 6 recite, in unison, the opening lines of Shakespeare's tragedy. 'Two households, both alike in dignity' . . .' They all know the words.

Romeo and Juliet seems particularly appropriate in Somers Town, another small community where families feud, honour is all and things can go tragically wrong for young people if adults let them down. There are masks hanging from the wall bars, each child has made their own, and they don them for the dance, singing along to Summer Love, hidden behind the gaudy faces they have made for themselves. It is Romeo and Juliet meets Grease and Craig has star quality, moving his hips, engaging the audience with his gaze. As narrator, he moves the story forward. 'Later that day, a brawl between the feuding families erupts again. . . .' When the Juliets serenade the Romeos on the bench-balcony, singing 'I'm hopelessly devoted to you', Collette can no longer hold back the tears.

With the show over, Seán recounts the story of Year 6, how they started (those of them who have been in the same school since nursery) as the school subsided and had to move into the Medburn Centre. How Ofsted came, and he was appointed head teacher all at the same time. How they came back to the school nearly a year later, and made it their home again. 'This will always be your school', he tells them. This Year 6 have come to maturity alongside him; they are his first generation of home-grown children.

Collette comes up to get her bouquet from the class; she has presents for every one of them – a book recording their two years with her and a T-shirt printed with a picture of the whole class, for signing. The boys dodge her kisses while Laura and Amy look on, wiping their eyes. Some of the girls are sniffing too.

Seán says goodbye not only to Year 6 but to several adults. The reading recovery teacher is going, as is the visiting art teacher; there is no longer the money in the budget to pay for their posts. Also gone is an ethnic minority support post, along with two assistants. Making these decisions has been 'horrendously difficult' for Seán and governors. 'Who wants to move backwards?' he asks. 'Offer a reduced level of service?'

* * *

After lunch, Purple nursery has its own mini-assembly. For nine of the children, it is their last day in Purple nursery – they are moving up or on. Najreen, tall and confident, has moved from being petrified to being completely at home in school. Popular with the other girls she chats in Bengali and her English is progressing rapidly. 'I'm writing for you my name', she tells Francisca, getting a piece of paper out of the handbag slung over her shoulder. And she does write her name, several times. It is hard to believe that this is the same child who used to throw herself against the glass of the nursery door when her mother left.

JoJo is leaving too, moving on to another school after five terms at Edith Neville. Nicki, his mother, likes the uniform and thinks their strict approach to discipline might suit him.

In a plastic crate in the office, his school life is contained in a yellow folder that will accompany him to his new school. His file records that when he started he liked colour games and jigsaw puzzles. That his friends were Rai and Joe and his targets for development 'to show care and concern for others' needs'. Here is one of his early drawings, a squiggly circle in purple felt pen. Several pages of yellow Post-its, all dated, record in Laura's writing his concentration in playing with the Hulk, his desire to be a policeman and his ability to name a range of vegetables. Amy's earlier notes record his anger when he made 'a mistake' in his drawing, and his statement that 'it was crap'. Later, she notes that JoJo is beginning to look at adults when speaking and becoming more confident to express his needs.

Under the personal development section, it records neutrally that 'JoJo threw lots of sand on the floor and at children. When I spoke to him, he laughed and spat at me.' 'JoJo has continued to hurt his friends.' That he has been tearful, kind, wanted his mum. His collages are here, and a photograph of him in his glasses, doing a jigsaw puzzle. His drawings take shape over the five terms he spends in Purple nursery. He moves from angry-looking tangles of lines to a Ninja turtle series, the two huge faces of mummy and daddy, then a long-running series on Spiderman, the criss-crossed lines increasingly sure and steady. Laura is there too, recognisable by her gold hoop ear-rings and red mouth.

The file records his anger management strategy devised by Shelagh and a list of the books he has borrowed to take home. The last comment is on the great progress he has made, 'especially in his emotional management'. Somehow, JoJo himself evades the information in his file.

Seán arrives to give out good attendance certificates. JoJo, who has only attended two-thirds of the time, does not get one but Sultan comes to collect his, and shakes Seán's hand, then Samir – Seán and

Nasima's son – who also shakes his father's hand. Samir has been voted by Purple nursery as their class representative to the school council.

When Seán has gone, the children gather on the carpet for a last story before going home. Staff are excited about the holidays too – Laura is going to Jamaica and Francisca to China. Several parents bring presents for the staff; they hug and kiss and promise to visit in the future. Francisca takes a last photo of each child, most of them holding up the red and gold good attendance certificates she made. Laura is crying again, her tears dripping on the floor. But when Nicki comes, she leaves her box of chocolates for the staff quietly by the pegs; caught up with cameras, tears and other parents, the staff do not notice her. JoJo slips out and is gone.

CODA

On May 16th 2005, seven years to the week since their last visit, Ofsted inspectors finally arrived at Edith Neville school. Initial impressions were broadly favourable; staff judged the inspectors 'fair' and 'experienced' during the first day of the inspection. Their assessments of the school were 'largely sound', said Seán O'Regan.

The Ofsted team learn on day two of their inspection that they too will be inspected while they are in the school – by HMI, the Chief Inspector's own full-time and highly senior inspectors. This means that some teachers will have to demonstrate their skills in front of one inspector being observed by another one. No one flinches.

On the third and final day, lead inspector Margaret Goodchild accompanies all the foundation stage children on a trip to the Science Museum. Sitting on the front seat of the coach, she is warm in her praise of the school. She hopes people realise, she says, that inspectors come in 'intending to be constructive'. She has already let Seán know that his leadership falls into the top category – excellent – as does Amy Crowther's work with the community. With a ratio of one adult for every single child, the visit to the museum goes off without a hitch.

Seán, after the team leaves, is exhausted. As a trained Ofsted inspector himself, and having led Edith Neville through an inspection before, he knows the ropes. A school must operate during inspection at top notch in every area, 'at a pitch that is unsustainable', he says.

With most staff working evenings and weekends in the run-up to the inspection, the school was in a state of high preparedness – from the planning in the files to the new shrubs in ceramic pots in the entrance area.

Still, the unexpected occurs. School keeper John Punton had to jump in a taxi to go and retrieve some forgotten files from a teacher's home one morning; Seán had to improvise an assembly when the assembly book vanished ten minutes before inspectors sat down to watch. More seriously, he had to demonstrate to inspectors how the cramped building constrains teaching, and dissect the figures to prove child by child that the fact that teacher assessments for the previous year's key stage 2 Sats were lower than students' actual results did not mean they had low expectations.

The report, when it comes, is glowing. Edith Neville is described as 'a highly effective school with a number of excellent features'. The inspectors note that the intake of children at Edith Neville is 'particularly disadvantaged and increasingly needy' and that their attainment on entry is very low. They say Seán 'has high aspirations and shows considerable flair' and that the school 'is exceptionally effective in its social inclusion of pupils with a significant level of need, and in the way it supports parents.' Science teaching is singled out for particular praise as is the promotion of racial harmony.

Ofsted recognises that results by the time children leave the school are well above the national average in science, and above average in maths. In English, results are still below the national average except when compared with 'similar schools' – when they are, more meaningfully, 'well above average'. The test system has no way of measuring the great achievements of children who, in most cases, began at Edith Neville primary school with almost no English and leave it with a fluent and easy grasp of the language.

Ninety-eight per cent of parents still agree or strongly agree that 'my child likes school'.